paint style

the new approach to decorative paint finishes

Lesley Riva

FIREFLY BOOKS

A FIREFLY BOOK

Published by Firefly Books Ltd. 2008

Copyright © 2008 Benjamin Moore & Co.

First printing

Publisher Cataloging-in-Publication Data (U.S.)

Riva, Lesley, 1964-
    Paint style : the new approach to decorative paint
finishes / Lesley Riva.
[176] p. : col. photos. ;   cm.
Includes index.
Summary: A step-by-step guide to basic and
advanced decorative paint techniques with dozens
of tips, advice and photographs of work by leading
interior designers and decorative painters. In-depth
advice on choosing colors and specific palettes
given for every technique by Benjamin Moore.
Information on new metallic and pearlescent paints,
and Venetian plasters; all instructions are for
environmentally friendly water-based paints.
ISBN-13: 978-1-55407-376-4
ISBN-10: 1-55407-376-6
1. House painting – Amateurs' manuals. 2. Texture
painting – Amateurs' manuals. 3. Interior walls
– Decoration – Amateurs' manuals. 4. Interior
decoration – Amateurs' manuals.   I. Title.
747/.3 dc22   TT323.R583 2008

**Library and Archives Canada Cataloguing in
Publication**

Riva, Lesley
    Paint style : the new approach to decorative
paint finishes / Lesley Riva.
Includes index.
ISBN-13: 978-1-55407-376-4
ISBN-10: 1-55407-376-6
        1. House painting. 2. Interior decoration.
3. Color in interior decoration. 4. Finishes and
finishing. I. Title.
TT323.R69 2008   747'.3   C2007-905657-1

Published in the United States by
Firefly Books (U.S.) Inc.
P.O. Box 1338, Ellicott Station
Buffalo, New York 14205

Published in Canada by
Firefly Books Ltd.
66 Leek Crescent
Richmond Hill, Ontario L4B 1H1

Printed in Singapore
Produced by Smallwood and Stewart, New York City

PAGE ONE

Venetian plaster
COLOR: Stardust 2108-40

PREVIOUS PAGE

A vibrant blue gives IMURI
Design's overscaled treatment
for a plain corner a pop feeling.
WALLS: Rocky Mountain Sky
2066-40
DESIGN: Bashful Blue 2065-70

OPPOSITE:

Designer James Lumsden used
color washing and stippling to
create an atmospheric backdrop for his collection of Spanish colonial art.
BASE: Wild Heart 1354
GLAZES: Cranberry Ice 1362,
Melrose Pink 1363

All decorative finishes on pages 62–159 were
produced by EverGreene Painting Studios, New
York City, except where noted.

Note: Printed colors can only approximate the color
of a coated chip. Use actual Benjamin Moore®
Color System chips when making a color selection.
Color names and numbers used throughout this
book refer to Benjamin Moore® Color Preview®,
Classic Colors®, or Affinity™.

Benjamin Moore, Color Preview, and the Triangle M
symbol, Benjamin Moore Classic Color Collection
are registered trademarks licensed to Benjamin
Moore & Co.

For information, write to Benjamin Moore & Co.,
Attn: Communications Department
101 Paragon Drive, Montvale, NJ 07645
www.benjaminmoore.com

MOTTLING
Page 65

STIPPLING
Page 67

RAGGING
Page 69

COLOR WASHING
Page 71

COMBING
Page 73

STRIÉ
Page 75

FLOOR STENCIL
Page 91

LATTICE DESIGN
Page 115

VENETIAN PLASTER
Page 127

contents

THIS PAGE
Copper stenciled pagodas
add a note of opulence to
this interior.
WALL: Huntington Green 406
STENCIL: Copper 40

OPPOSITE
A painted color field can do
wonders to emphasize and
flatter artwork, particularly
when the color is pulled from
the art itself. The deep red
of the wagon wheels on this
quilt almost glows against the
painted "frame," adding
to its impact.
WALL PANEL: Ravishing Red
2008-10

how to use this book

The power of color to transform a room is familiar to anyone who's picked up a paint brush. Going one step further and using a decorative finish adds a whole new dimension: Classic stries can produce a look like raw silk, color washing contributes a cloudy depth to the color, and, of course, faux finishes can simulate everything from marble and stone to fine woods. Today, decorative painting encompasses these advanced finishes and something as simple as an overscaled stencil design or a series of stripes in contrasting colors. PAINT STYLE shows you both classic and contemporary possibilities with paint and color, and gives you the techniques and even the colors to enable you to produce these effects.

Any successful decorative finish begins with good colors. "Good color" is highly subjective, but we've provided some guidelines to help you arrive at the pale blues or lilacs, creams or rich browns, sage greens or teals that will appeal to you. Then, we've gathered the best work from leading professionals to inspire and show you what some of the most popular finishes look like in "real life."

In the step-by-steps, we give instructions, tips, and specific colors for techniques that are building blocks—used separately or in combination, they will enable you to create a huge array of looks. But, in the end, decorative painting is as much art as craft and best mastered by hands-on practice. How much color you mix in the glaze or how you apply it to the wall varies from painter to painter and the results vary correspondingly. Sometimes the mistakes turn out to be happy ones. Ultimately, the best approach is to pick up a brush, experiment and discover the power of color and decorative painting for yourself.

A crisp graphic wall treatment in a New York City apartment is simplicity itself. With nothing more than two painted white lines on a black background, the homeowners have conjured up a headboard and created "architectural" interest where there was none.
WALL COLOR: Black 2132-10
STRIPES: White

Traditional New England farmhouses, like this circa 1800 Connecticut home, often used stenciling rather than more costly wallpaper to brighten a room. Versatile and relatively easy and fast to execute, stenciling reflected the early-nineteenth-century taste for elaborate and fanciful painted decoration throughout the home.

introduction

Like fine cooking, decorative painting transforms a basic necessity into art. A plain coat of white paint on the walls could certainly suffice, yet we prefer to introduce colors and patterns and combine them in a way that flatters the space and pleases us. And sometimes we go further, revitalizing a nondescript dining room with a stenciled border, or igniting a dim stairwell with a glowing color wash, because to personalize a space with a decorative finish is to infuse the mundane with style and character.

Of course, faux and decorative effects have their practical aspects as well. An elaborate color grid distracts the eye from awkward room proportions; a patterned ceiling draws in a soaring space and makes it feel cozier. A mottled glaze might camouflage a damaged surface, and wood graining and marbling give inexpensive materials the look of something far more precious.

But at heart, decorative painting isn't about solving problems. It's about the simple pleasure of creating something beautiful. And that aesthetic attraction—the impulse to embellish and modify our surroundings—is as old as humankind. From prehistoric times, we began painting on walls from the very moment we had walls to paint on. The startlingly sure-handed animal scenes found in caves around the world, from Lascaux, France, and Cantabria, Spain, to Thailand and Australia, may have had a concrete purpose—to influence the hunt, give thanks for a harvest, or fulfill a religious ritual. But anyone seeing them now can sense an aesthetic element as well: Some unknown artist paused in his or her struggle for survival and took the time to create something lovely to look at.

As societies developed, so did the scale of their artistic endeavors. The ancient Egyptians were masters of interior color, painting the walls of tombs (and most probably palaces and other structures) with elaborate figural murals and decorative motifs. In China and India, skilled artisans filled temples with intricate painted designs and portrayals of Hindu divinities or, later, the Buddha. And although we think of Greek temples and monuments as being defined by the purity of spare white marble and classical lines, these ancient structures were once brightly colored. Temple columns and capitals were painted in vivid reds and blues or embellished with gold leaf and black detailing; only time has stripped them down to the underlying stone.

The Romans took their cue from the Greeks and decorated both public buildings and private residences. The vast swaths of society that were preserved under the ashes and lava at Pompeii and Herculaneum give us a firsthand view of the sophisticated murals and decorative detail employed throughout the two communities. Private villas were filled with artistic motifs, from trompe l'oeil fountains to marbleized columns, while elaborate figurative murals were "framed" with painted architectural friezes.

In Europe throughout the Middle Ages, the decorative arts were used mostly in service of the Church to produce religious scenes and icons for worship, and to illustrate biblical themes for a largely illiterate population. Islamic painters, forbidden by religious edict to create images, developed their own distinctive style using elaborate patterns and colors. Palaces, homes of the wealthy, and mosques throughout the Ottoman empire were adorned with brilliant ornamentation.

By the Renaissance, Italian artists had begun to perfect the fresco—painting on wet lime plaster—which allowed them to cover broad areas of walls and ceilings with glowing color and naturalistic technique. Churches, chapels, and even private residences were overlaid with gorgeous frescoes, and purely decorative effects such as marbling and faux architectural detail again became common. Aristocrats grew ever more extravagant, and a veritable army of artists trained in gold leafing, stenciling, fresco, and other decorative finishes was enlisted to grace their homes. The palace complex at Versailles, conceived of as a showplace of French arts and crafts, is often thought of as the zenith of this kind of gilded opulence, its acres of rococo interiors highly influential throughout Europe for generations.

As new trade routes opened to China, India, and the New World, exotic materials, particularly tropical hardwoods, filtered back to Europe. In eighteenth-century England, for example, the great manor houses were filled with prized woods such as mahogany from the island of Santo Domingo. But these exotic woods were too costly for most, so techniques to simulate them were developed for use in more modest homes and buildings.

Some of these new skills and styles followed European settlers as they struck out for America's shores. In the beginning, colonial structures were few and humble, but evidence is emerging that many early homes were decorated with painted ceilings, black-

Rufus Porter, an itinerant artist, inventor, and publisher, painted dozens of murals throughout New England in the early 1800s, often depicting common scenes of the new nation. This detail is from a restored Porter mural in the Moses Mason house in Bethel, Maine.

banded baseboards, and broad stripes to define the perimeter of a fireplace. The 1664 Gedney House in Salem, Massachusetts, for example, was recently discovered to have extensive decorative detailing, with beams and other features picked out in a vivacious green paint. Sponge painting was also popular, executed by dipping a sponge into lamp-black (literally the soot from candles or oil lamps) and making small dots on a whitewashed wall. Later, as a prosperous commercial society took shape, wandering artisans with little formal training in fine arts techniques would exchange their services in decorative or mural painting for a square meal and a warm bed. Itinerant painters such as Rufus Porter painted elaborate murals in hundreds of New England homes throughout the early nineteenth century. His work, a mix of stencil and freehand painting, was widely sought after, and existing examples, such as the Reed Homestead in Massachusetts and the Daniel Carr House in New Hampshire, are regarded as museum pieces. Hezekiah Reynolds, another traveling artisan, wrote one of the first "how-to" books for American decorative painters in 1812. In it he shared formulas for mixing paints and colors, as well as directions on floor painting, including diamond patterns, floral borders, and floor cloths.

By the early nineteenth century, stenciling and all manner of decorative painting was popular even in modest homes, adding color and energy to plain, often poorly lit rooms and ornamentation to the humblest household items. Immigrants, bringing folk art traditions and motifs from their homelands, decorated furniture, tableware, and tools as well as walls with cheerful designs, such as well-loved Pennsylvania Dutch motifs of hearts, tulips, birds, and the like. Marbling, both naturalistic and colorfully freeform, and wood-graining techniques were also widely used on both furniture and wall surfaces. Vinegar painting, which involved a glaze made of vinegar, sugar, water, and pigment, was used to create an extraordinary variety of faux grains and more elaborate patterns on chests, cupboards, and interior woodwork. Some of the popularity of these techniques was rooted in economics—through the early part of the nineteenth century, wallpaper was taxed by the British government, pushing up prices. But at the same time, there was also a vogue for fanciful and imaginative decoration of everything from fabrics to furniture.

The Victorian age was marked by a taste for ever-more meticulous wood graining: Marvelously precise imitations of fine hardwoods were painted on everything from inexpensive pine furniture to wall paneling and woodwork. The early years of the twentieth century saw the explosion of art nouveau, with its elaborate wall ornamentation featuring lush, flowing floral borders and freehand design. In the 1930s, a revived interest in large-scale public murals was fed by Franklin Roosevelt's WPA, which put unemployed artists to work painting detailed scenes in courthouses, post offices, and other public buildings.

Today, decorative finishes are undergoing yet another revival, as people lavish time and attention on their homes, creating comforting, personalized retreats from an increasingly impersonal and frenetic world. In a landscape of sprawling subdivisions

This exuberant parlor in the historic San Francisco Plantation House in southeastern Louisiana, decorated around 1856, covers almost the entire range of decorative and faux finishes in one room. The fireplace is made of cypress, painted to look like azure marble; the ceiling medallion and borders are dressed with gilding, stenciling, and freehand design; the doors and transoms are treated with wood-graining techniques to simulate tiger oak.

and multiplying condominiums, decorative effects can help confer instant age and patina on brand-new construction and add interest to cookie-cutter architecture. Deep glazes and textured effects also feed the contemporary interest in changeable, mutable finishes, colors that shift and morph with the changing light and mood of a room. And decorative painting allows us to incorporate global influences from an ever-smaller planet, where the colors and styles of India, Morocco, Sweden, Mexico, and China, to name just a few countries, are an integral part of our visual world.

In the end, decorative painting has endured because it is, simply put, a joyous artistic endeavor, as close as some of us will ever come to experiencing the artist's delight in creating. So if you've picked up this book as the prelude to a project, take your time—and take pleasure in the process. Don't expect to complete an entire room on one Sunday afternoon. Plan carefully and execute practice samples until you're confident with your chosen technique. Make sure that the room you're working in is well lit and that you have the right equipment on hand. Step back frequently to get some perspective on how the total effect looks. And most of all, enjoy yourself.

A fabulous Audubon-esque flamingo is part of an oversize mural that stretches across the central hall of a restored Virginia plantation, up the stairs and around a second-floor landing. The design, created by noted costume jewelry maker Kenneth Jay Lane, was inspired by historic Zuber panoramic wallpapers. The claw-foot settee is early nineteenth century. In a bit of playful trompe l'oeil, its green upholstery seems shaded by the green limbs of the painted willow overhead.

1

color

Color's power to shape the way we feel about a room is almost magical. Consciously or unconsciously, very often it's the first thing we notice. The wrong color can almost literally repel us, whereas the right color will immediately draw us in. Color has the power to add character to a dull space, soften a harsh one, make a room feel warm or cold, intimate or expansive.

Yet finding the right color can be challenging for even the most experienced designer. Our taste in color is so personal and, because a given color will look quite different depending on its setting, it's almost impossible to provide anything beyond general guidelines.

THE COLOR WHEEL

A little bit of color theory, however, can go a long way in narrowing down your choices and helping you make ones you won't want to paint over. Enter the color wheel, which provides a simple way of arranging colors and illustrating their relationships one to another (see page 24). This is especially helpful with decorative painting, which often involves layering more than one color or shade.

Using the color wheel, colors can be divided into primary, secondary, and tertiary groupings. Primary colors—red, yellow, and blue—are those from which all other colors can be made. Secondary colors are made by combining two primary colors: Blue and red make purple; red and yellow make orange; yellow and blue make green. Tertiary colors are made by combining one primary and one secondary color: yellow and green make yellow-green; blue and green make blue-green, and so on.

Visually, the color wheel shows us how colors relate to one another. Analogous colors—those next to each other on the color wheel—are natural partners, creating a low-contrast, calm, mellow effect: Picture green with turquoise or blue with violet, for example.

A cheeky color grid floats above a bookcase, mirroring the blocky shapes and colorful titles of the volumes below. The mix of shades works well together because the colors are all equally bright, with the neutral squares of taupe serving as a bridge between hues.
SQUARES FROM TOP LEFT:
Clearspring Green HC-128,
Avon Green HC-126,
Golden Bark 2153-10,
Redstone 2009-10,
Blueberry 2063-30,
Coyote Trail 1224,
Putnam Ivory HC-39,
Hasbrouck Brown HC-71,
Pumpkin Cream 2168-20,
Kingsport Gray HC-86,
Santa Monica Blue 776,
Alexandria Beige HC-77

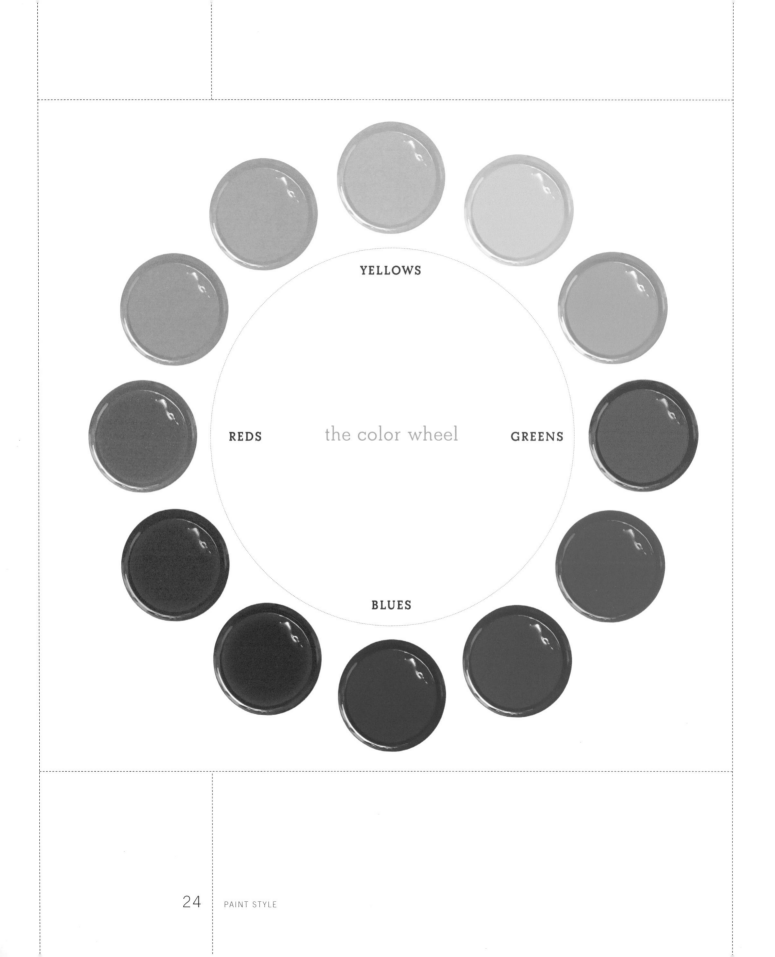

YELLOWS

REDS the color wheel GREENS

BLUES

In contrast, complementary colors—colors directly opposite each other on the color wheel—enhance one another by making each look brighter and more intense. Complementary pairs set up tension—they look almost as if they're vibrating—so they usually work best when one color dominates and the other is used sparingly as an accent. An orange pillow will pop out against a Wedgwood blue wall; a red rug will give a jolt to an emerald-green room.

Monochromatic colors are simply different shades of the same color, so by nature they tend to be harmonious: Layering a room in varying shades of brown, from cream to coffee to caramel, has a subtle, calm, and sophisticated feel.

Another way to analyze the color wheel is to draw a line through it with the red, orange, and yellow color families on one side. These are considered warm colors, with their ties to earth, heat, and sun. And, on the other side, the blues, greens, and purples—the cool colors of sky, leaves, and water. In general, warm colors tend to pair best with warm, and cool with cool.

Of course, most colors around us are not as pure as those shown on the color wheel, which are at their most intense, or "saturated." Often they contain some white, which makes them "tints" (a pale blue is a tint of blue); some gray, which makes them "tones" (sage green is a grayed version of green); or some black, which makes them "shades" (dark red is a shade of red). And they almost always contain a little of another color altogether—chocolate browns can contain a little red or blue; pinks can have a cool blue component, such as shocking pinks, or warm orange ones—like corals or salmon pinks. These underlying colors can provide further

clues to finding successful partners. Among greens, for example, yellow-greens, such as lime, olive, and fern, are warmed by the presence of yellow—and will tend to pair better with yellows. Blue-greens, such as aqua and teal, feel cool because they contain a great deal of blue themselves; these will pair better with blues. Learning to identify these components in the colors you're considering makes pairings easier—a blue-gray, for example, will partner better with a blue than with a reddish gray or even a green-gray.

COMBINING COLORS

A successful decorative finish—whether stippling or a color wash or a stenciled border—relies almost as much on good color pairing as it does on mastery of a technique. While there's really no substitute for trying out different combinations, here are some guidelines to help you narrow down your choices:

• A base color and a glaze color in the same family but in different values (their relative lightness or darkness) is always a safe choice. The combed pattern on page 72 is a good example of this.

• The lower the contrast between the base coat and the glaze coat—that is, the closer the colors are in value (how light or dark they appear)—the more subtle and soft the result: An example is the almost tone-on-tone effect of the stippled finish on page 66.

• The greater the contrast between the base coat and glaze coat—that is, the farther apart the colors are in value—the more vibrant and active the effect.

• Very often, a lighter glaze over a darker base coat will tend to feel cooler.

• For the most part, a darker glaze over a

lighter base coat will tend to feel warmer and more inviting.

THE THEORY OF RELATIVITY

Even with these very general guidelines, bear in mind that color is a chameleon, changing with its surroundings and the light.

As light moves from dawn to dusk or season to season, the appearance of the colors in our rooms changes along with it, often in radical ways. The pale blue of a bedroom may look silvery in the morning, fade almost to white in strong afternoon sun, and turn flat and gray in the evening. A simple white wall may look green in summer light filtered through verdant foliage but gray in flat winter light, when leaves have fallen and skies are overcast.

Similarly, artificial light in our homes also affects the way we see colors. Most table lamps are incandescent and cast a warm, yellowish light. Like halogen lights, they enhance reds and yellows and dull down blues and greens. Fluorescents tend to be cooler, so they have the opposite effect—strengthening blues and greens and dulling down reds and yellows.

For all these reasons, it's essential to look at colors in the light in which they'll be used. The moss greens and slate grays that looked so attractive in a friend's country home or, for that matter, in the paint store, might look totally unappealing in the very different light and context of a sun-filled beach cottage.

As much as color is affected by light, it is also powerfully shaped by scale and context. The larger the area of color, the more intense it will appear—the bright, bouncy orange that makes a tiny powder room hum with energy would be overwhelming if it covered all four living room walls. Very pale colors can suffer a reverse effect: A gossamer blue that looks strong on a small color chip may be barely noticeable when stretched out over a ceiling. Then, try placing it next to a bright turquoise and it will appear even paler.

MAKING CHOICES

It's this highly mutable nature of color, coupled with the seemingly limitless options—paint stores typically carry about three thousand choices and can match nearly any shade from a swatch—that can make the search such a challenge. In the end, the "right" choice for any room is simply the shade of red—or green or brown or blue—that appeals to you. And to find it, there's really no substitute for trying out actual colors where you'll be using them; even the most experienced designer is never entirely sure how a color will look until it is up on the walls of the room and seen in the context of its furnishings.

So how do you go about choosing the specific colors to use in your home? To start focusing your ideas, ask yourself the following questions:

What mood do I want to create? Color can help set the emotional tone of a room, from warm and enveloping to brisk and breezy. A smoky taupe can confer a cozy, protective feel suitable for a den where you curl up in the evening; pastels such as a fresh periwinkle make a breakfast room feel bright, bracing, and invigorating; muted, complex colors such as a soft sage work for a study where a calm, unhurried atmosphere is good for concentration and relaxation.

• *What space do I have?* A small room can suddenly feel spacious if bathed all over in a single

Dominic Fusco designed this Venetian Plaster mural using bold colors to give this show house home gym a shot of energy in keeping with its purpose. Furnishings, window treatments, and carpet were restricted to black and white so as not to compete with the vibrant, Mondrian-inspired graphics.

COLORS:
Surf Blue 2056-30,
Rosemary Green 2029-30,
Rockies Brown 2107-30,
Tangy Orange 2014-30

pale color that erases the distinctions between walls and ceiling. A dark color can create a sophisticated, nighttime look. A light shade can give a low ceiling extra lift. Contrasting end walls can break up a boxy space. A long narrow hallway can be transformed by painting one far wall a darker color (darker colors appear to advance).

What colors do I already have in the room? From fabrics to floor to fireplace, your home is full of color before you ever begin to paint. Take those "given" colors into account when you try to devise your color scheme: The background color in a rug may look fabulous on the wall, accented with other shades drawn from the weave; the golden wood of your floor or the gray stone from your mantelpiece may prompt you to pair them with other earth tones; the dark Asian antiques in your dining room may cry out for a striking red backdrop.

Taking context into account also means looking at the surrounding spaces and rooms. If the room you are working on is open to an adjacent space, bear in mind the colors in that room.

What is the setting? Look outside the window and take your cue from the view. A leafy, rural landscape may suggest a range of greens, browns, and golds. A seaside setting can be carried inside with a palette of watery blues and greens.

What's the available light? Both natural and artificial light have an enormous influence on how your color choices will "read." Dark colors such as charcoal gray, chocolate brown, and forest green need strong light; in low light, they may simply look black. On the other hand, strong light may wash out a delicate blue or pastel pink; it may be better to save them for a room that's not bathed in sunlight most of the day. Another piece of standard advice—no less true for being oft repeated—is to check your exposure: South-facing rooms can sometimes benefit from a dose of cool color, while north-facing rooms may need warm colors to turn up the visual temperature.

And the best advice of all? Make your color choices in the room where they will be used. Take color chips home from the paint store and look at them next to fabrics and furnishings, in daylight and at night. (When you're combining colors for a decorative effect, make sure to collect chips for all the shades you're considering.) Better yet, ask your paint retailer for an oversize chip; many stores stock large-scale color cards that you can borrow for a few days.

PRACTICE, PRACTICE

In the end, there's no substitute for experimentation, especially with glazing. In any technique where two or more colors are being combined it's difficult to anticipate how they'll look together. (Professionals will sometimes glaze large pieces of Mylar to hold against different base colors.) Always paint samples (on poster board) not just to find the right colors but also to get a feel for the technique—how easy or hard it is and how to handle the brush or other tools.

Once you've completed samples, take the time to observe them. If this is a room where you spend lots of time at night, how do the colors look by lamplight? Do they stand up to the morning sun, or fade to mud at dusk? How do they relate to your furniture and rugs? Only when you've lived with the samples for a day or two and feel happy with your choices should you move on to painting the entire project.

choosing a palette

There may be thousands of choices in a fan deck or on display at your paint store, but our color vocabulary is surprisingly limited. What do we mean when we say we want a pale blue room? Do we really mean azure? robin's egg? To help you understand what you really want, on the following pages we've broken out the main color families, shown you the range of possibilities within each—warms versus cools, darks versus lights, grayed versus saturated—and paired them with actual paint colors. Now you can see at a glance what your options are, make comparisons easily, and turn directly to the paints that best exemplify your preferences.

PURE OR "CLEAN" WHITES are formulated without any undertones to tint the finished coat. A favorite of designers looking for a backdrop to showcase art and furnishings, they include White; Super White; Decorators White; Vapor AF-35; Deep in Thought AF-3;, Frostine AF-5; Gardenia AF-10.

BLUE-GREEN WHITES have a cool, crisp, breezy feel and blend well with equally cool colors from the blue and green side of the spectrum. These whites include Seafoam 2123-60; Wedding Veil 2125-70; Winter White 2140-70; Mineral Ice 2132-70; White Diamond OC-61; Patriotic White 2135-70; White Ice 2139-70; Snow White 2122-70; Ice Mist 2123-7; Constellation AF-540.

PINK WHITES have a subtle rose or peachy blush that is flattering to faces and furnishings alike. They include Antique White as well as Soft White 2170-70; Mirage White 2116-70; Oyster 2115-70; Shell Pink 883; Ambrosia 893; Pink Essence 881; Moonlight White OC-125; Pink Damask 890; Mystical Powers 901; Mauve Hint 878; Opal OC-73; Old Fashioned Peach OC-79; Parchment OC-78; Mascarpone AF-20.

YELLOW WHITES are often described as warm, creamy, or buttery. These whites include Linen White, Navajo White, Cameo White; Mayonnaise 2152-70; Lemon Ice 2024-70; Antique Yellow OC-103; Deserted Island OC-99; Cream Froth OC-97; Lychee AF-40; Collector's Item AF-45; Hush AF-95; Ylang Ylang AF-305.

WHITES come in a staggering variety of shades. A pure or "clean" white, which contains no deep pigments or toning of any sort, is the whitest. Most others can be divided into two families: warm whites, with yellow, pink, or brownish undertones, and cool whites, with minty green or blue-gray undertones.

GRAYS

are the chameleons of color—infinitely adaptable, at home in any color scheme. They always blend in and take on some of their neighbor's complementary shade: Gray next to red will look green; gray next to green will look red. This quality makes gray a true neutral, able to fade into the background and complement any decor.

VIOLET-GRAYS reveal a dusky, amethyst tinge. Colors include Silver Dollar 1460; Sea Life 2118-40; Heaven 2118-70; Misty Memories 2118-60; Winter Gray 2117-60; Dreamy Cloud 2117-70; Full Moon 2119-70; Instinct AF-57; Wisteria AF-585.

BLUE-GRAYS have a cool, silvery, metallic quality. Colors in this family: Smoke 2122-40; Little Falls 1621; Manor Blue 1627; New Hope Gray 2130-50; Winter Lake 2129-50; Misty Gray 2124-60, Marilyn's Dress 2125-60; Silver Half Dollar 2121-40; Deep Silver 2124-30; Solitude AF-545; Serenata AF-535; Eternity AF-695; Storm AF-700.

TRUE GRAYS are the pale value of black, without colored undertones. Often used as an alternative to black, they make a crisp, lower-contrast pairing with white. They include Silver Lake 1598; Boothbay Gray HC-165; Seattle Gray 2130-70; Mineral Ice 2132-70; Sterling 1591; Cobblestone Path 1606; Rock Gray 1615; Wish AF-680; Nightingale AF-670.

MUTABLE AND COMPLEX, GREEN-GRAYS can have a warm, sagebrush glow or a cool, water-in-winter look. Colors include Raindance 1572; Salisbury Green HC-139; Homestead Green AC-19; Cedar Mountains 706; Antique Jade 465; Quarry Rock 1568; Carolina Gull 2138-40; Green Tint 2139-60; Flora AF-470; Croquet AF-455; Tranquility AF-490.

OLIVE AND PUTTY GRAYS can be a bridge color between warm and cooler shades, revealing hints of deep green and brown. In this family: Hampshire Gray HC-101; Providence Olive HC-98; Victorian Garden 1531; Spanish Olive 1509; November Rain 2142-60; Antique Pewter 1560; October Mist 1495; Rockport Gray HC-105; Castle Peak Gray, 1561; Lapland AF-410; Elemental AF-400.

THE SOFT GRAYS have yellow, taupe, and beige notes. Colors may include Waynesboro Taupe 1544; Sag Harbor Gray HC-95; Silver Fox 2108-50; Cumulus Cloud 1550; Vapor Trails 1556; Richmond Gray HC-96; Winter Orchard 1555; Seattle Mist 1535; Thunder AF-685; Pashmina AF-100.

BROWN-GRAYS have a warm, rich quality. Colors include Smoked Oyster 2109-40; Chelsea Gray HC-168; Stardust 2108-40; Fieldstone 1558; Nimbus 1465; Light Pewter1464; Equestrian Gray 1553; Gray Huskie 1473; Coastal Fog 976; River Reflections 1552; Weimeraner AF-155; Dolphin AF-715; Sparrow AF-720.

PURPLE-BROWNS have deep notes of cinnamon and burgundy—think of mocha and mauve. Colors include Townsend Harbor Brown HC-64; Bison Brown 2113-30; Incense Stick 2115-20; Wisp of Mauve 2098-60; Cinnamon Slate 2113-40; Café Ole 2098-40; Early Sunset 2096-70; Wild Rice 2097-70; Caponata AF-650; Wenge AF-180; French Press AF-170.

REDDISH- OR ORANGE-BROWNS can range from rusty shades of brick and clay to light melon colors. These colors can be a good choice when you want a warm shade but are uncomfortable with bright red. In this family: Harvest Moon 2167-30; Baked Terra Cotta 1202; Georgian Brick HC-50; Mexican Tile 1194; Baker's Dozen 1216; Corslbud Canyon 076; Jumel Peachtone HC-54; Antique Coral 1198; Buttered Yam AF-230; Masada AF-220; Italianate AF-215.

LEATHERY SHADES OF TAN range from frothy cappuccino to nut brown. Some shades have a coppery undertone. Colors include Saddle Tan 1124; Marsh Brown 2164-20; Tawny 2161-20; Penny 2163-30; Burlap 2163-50; Adobe Beige 1128; Plymouth Brown HC-73; Havana Tan 1121; October Sky 2162-70; Lambskin 1051; Satchel AF-240; Warmed Cognac AF-235; Rustique AF-275.

GOLDEN BROWNS have strong yellow undertones and range from pale ivory to burnished bronze. Colors include Peanut Butter 2159-20; Golden Dunes 2157-10; Apple Crisp 2159-30; Stuart Gold HC-10; Hathaway Gold 194; Bryant Gold HC-7; Camel 2165-10; Straw 2154-50; Key West Ivory 192; Old Gold 167; Turmeric AF-350; Citrine AF-370; Etruscan AF-355.

BEIGE-BROWNS have a warm, creamy quality that makes them versatile neutrals. Colors in this family: Shelburne Buff HC-28; Dunmore Cream HC-29; Lighthouse Landing 1044; Quincy Tan HC-25; Powell Buff HC-35; Waterbury Cream HC-31; Philadelphia Cream HC-30; Monroe Bisque HC-26; Safari AF-335; Subtle AF-310; Jicama AF-315.

YELLOW-BROWNS sometimes have olive undertones, making them a natural bridge between yellows and greens. Colors include Brazen 259; Corduroy 2153-20; Livingston Gold HC-16; Princeton Gold HC-14; Norfolk Cream 261; Woven Jacquard 254; Henderson Buff HC-15; Timothy Straw 2149-40; Thyme 2148-20; Sombrero 249; Rattan AF-375; Anjou Pear AF-425; Elemental AF-400.

TAUPES OR GRAY-BROWNS contain a lot of gray, making them easily adaptable partners for other colors, particularly grayed shades that share the same values. Colors in this family: Free Spirit 245; Rustic Taupe 999; Northampton Putty HC-89; Hampshire Taupe 990; Stone House 1039; Brandy Cream 1030; Litchfield Gray HC-78; Greenbrier Beige HC-79; Elk Horn AF-105; Coriander Seed AF-110; Truffle AF-130; Morrel AF-125.

BROWNS, full of nuance and depth, run from the rich, appetizing shades of chocolate and cinnamon to the calming tones of buff, taupe, and sand. Though their paler guises are often used to anchor neutral color schemes, the zestier shades of bronze, copper, and caramel are great on walls and trim as well. Used on a large scale, deep browns work best in rooms with abundant light, where the color reads true without shading to black.

GREEN,
the easiest color for the eye to see, is often thought of as calming and restful, though its more acidic, citrusy shades certainly pack a lively punch. Because it falls between blue and yellow on the color wheel, it's a good bridge color that pairs well with both warm and cool palettes. Silvery sages, citrus greens, and dark, historic greens have seen a recent rise in popularity.

OLIVE AND ALLIGATOR GREENS have brownish undertones. Colors include Jalapeno Pepper 2147-30; Avon Green HC-126; Olive Moss 2147-20; Mesquite 501; Sweet Daphne 529; Olive Branch 2143-30; Sherwood Green HC-118; Agave AF-420; Wasabi AF-430.

YELLOW-GREENS can range from the famous avocado to acidic chartreuse. Colors in this category include Avocado 2145-10; Limesickle 2145-50; Split Pea 2146-30; Brookside Moss 2145-30; Soft Fern, 2144-40; Dried Parsley, 522; Chartreuse, 2024-10; Citron, 2024-30; Pale Sea Mist 2147-50.

LIME AND APPLE GREENS have a bright, contemporary feeling. Colors include Margarita 2026-20; Tequila Lime 2028-30; Dark Lime 2027-10; Fresh Cut Grass 2026-50; Summer Lime 2026-60; Garland Green 429; Neon Celery 2031-60; Willow Springs Green 418; Paradise Green 2031-20.

KELLY GREENS, GRASS GREENS, AND EMERALDS include Fresh Scent Green 2033-30; Jade Green 2037-20; Emerald Isle 2039-20; Four Leaf Clover 573; Leprechaun Green 557; Lotus Flower 571; Acadia Green 2034-50; Marina Bay 2036-50; Kelly Green 2037-30; Light Pistachio 2034-60.

WARMER DEEP GREENS range from dark hunter green (a popular accent color) to light shades of eucalyptus. In low light, the deepest shades may read as black. Colors include Nile Green 2035-30; Ming Jade 2043-20; Forest Green 2041-10; Deep Sea 623; Key Largo Green 620; Capri Seas 2047-40; Italian Ice Green 2035-70; Antigua Aqua 610; Lido Green 617; Boreal Forest AF-480; Lush AF-475.

TEAL-GREENS include aquas and have an intense, almost luminous quality. Colors include Amelia Island Blue 2044-40; Coastal Paradise 655; Harbourside Teal 654; Bahama Green 2045-40; Blue Spa 2052-40; Caribbean Cool 661; Sea of Green 657; Hannity Green 646.

GRAY-GREENS in this grouping are cooled with hints of blue. Colors include Everglades 641; Aberdeen Green 631; Fresh Dew 435; Scenic Drive 697; Norway Spruce 452; Garden Oasis 699; Forest Valley Green 634; Georgian Green HC-115; Waterbury Green HC-136; Covington Blue HC-138; Urban Nature AF-440; Aventurine AF-445; Seedling AF-450.

BLUE-GRAYS are a low-intensity alternative to brighter blues, delivering the cool color in a less vivid form. Colors include Niagara Falls 1657; Alfresco 1672; Hemlock 719; Old Blue Jeans 839; Whipple Blue HC-152; Mediterranean Sky 1662; Marlboro Blue HC-153; Polar Ice 1660; Glacier Blue 1653; Amsterdam AF-550; Atmospheric AF-500; Exhale AF-515.

PALE, WATERY BLUES still have a hint of green; its shades feel gauzy and fresh. Colors include Delano Waters 766; San Clemente Teal 730; Sapphire Ice 808; Splash 2059-60; Crystal Springs 764; Mystical Blue 792; Little Boy Blue 2061-60; Breath of Fresh Air 806; Constellation AF-540.

TEAL-BLUES AND TURQUOISE-BLUES are almost equal parts green and blue and have a tropical feeling. Colors include Palm Coast Teal 733; Blue Lagoon 2054-40; Cool Aqua 2056-40; Seaside Resort 725; Seaside Blue 2054-50; Turquoise Powder 2057-50; Innocence 2055-70; Clear Skies 2054-70; Icy Moon Drops 2056-70.

ROYAL BLUES BUILD on a deep, primary blue base. Lighter shades are the classic powder blue and baby blue. In this family: Ol' Blue Eyes 2064-30; Dark Royal Blue 2065-20; Midnight Navy 2067-10; Toronto Blue 2060-40; Light Blue 2066-70; Blue Marguerite 2063-50; Athens Blue 797; Bluebelle 2064-60.

PERIWINKLE OR LAVENDER BLUES are warmed by notes of red and violet. Colors include Brazilian Blue 817; Blue Pearl 1433; Spring Flowers 1430; Lavender Blue 1438; Violet Dusk 1409; Misty Blue 820; Aqua Marina 816; Sweet Bluette 813; Luxe AF-580; Wisteria AF-585.

VIOLET, LILAC, LAVENDER are lighter, cooler violets influenced more by blue than by red. Violet is another effective "bridge" color, working well with both cool and warm palettes. Colors include Seduction 1399; Persian Violet 1419; English Hyacinth 1417; French Lilac 1403; Lavender Mist 2070-60; Spring Lilac 1388; Lily Lavender 2071-60; Nosegay 1401; Inspired AF-595; Amorous AF-600.

PURPLES AND PLUMS are very powerful, warm colors, sometimes bordering on pink in their lighter notes. Colors include Twilight Magenta 2074-30; Pink Raspberry 2075-40; Summer Plum 2074-20; Plum Perfect 1371; Purple Easter Egg 2073-50; Passion Pink 2075-60; Luscious 1369; Kalamata AF-630; Bonne Nuit AF-635; Aplomb AF-625.

BLUE

is often cited as America's favorite color. Quintessentially cool—the color of ice, snow, and water—blues also offer warmer variations as they move toward the lavender end of the spectrum. Pair blue with greens and minty whites for an icy, refreshing palette; spike it with dashes of a complementary red or yellow to warm or enliven its coolness.

RED

always makes a statement. In its lighter, brighter incarnations, it is energetic, powerful, stimulating. In its darker tones, it feels rich, warm, and luxurious. Saturated jewel tones of hot pink and magenta add sophisticated style and sparkle to a decor, while coral and salmon tones evoke tropical climates. Deep reds are a good choice in rooms used by night, such as formal dining rooms.

VIOLET-REDS are often described as magenta, orchid, and fuchsia. Lighter tones include airy baby pinks and roses, while darker tones have an exotic, feminine punch. In this family: Gypsy Pink 2077-20; Peony 2079-30; Cranberry Ice 1362; Raspberry Mousse 2076-40; Paradise Pink 2078-40; I Love You Pink 2077-70; Peppermint 1359.

BURGUNDY AND CRANBERRY shades often feel at home in historic or traditional interiors. Colors include Cranberry Cocktail 2083-20; Plum Raisin 2082-20; Gypsy Love 2085-30; Rosewood 2082-40; Rose Rococo 1275; Powder Blush 1388; Tara 1270; Caliente AF-290; Dinner Party AF-300.

BRIGHT BUBBLEGUM PINKS have many gradations, from the little-girl pink of ballet slippers to powerful pink Popsicle. Cooler than strong reds, these pinks still read as warm. In this family are Bubble Bath 1326; True Pink 2003-40; Springtime Bloom 2079-40; Pink Lace 2081-60; Cat's Meow 1332; Pink Eraser 2005-50; Marshmallow Bunny 2001-7;Head Over Heels AF-250; Fondant AF-255.

BRIGHT REDS are very strong colors best used in small doses or as an accent. Colors include Red 2000-10; Candy Cane Red 2079-10; Raspberry Truffle 2080-10; Mediterranean Spice 1337; Cherry Wine 2080-30; Confederate Red 2080-20; Cactus Flower 1335.

SALMON PINKS AND CORAL REDS contain a lot of orange, giving them a peachy complexion. Colors include Tucson Coral 005; Passion Fruit 2171-40; Perky Peach 2012-50; Bermuda Pink 016; Coral Reef 012; Sunlit Coral 2170-60; Salmon Peach 2013-50; Dusk Pink 2013-40.

RUST REDS AND OCHERS have deep brown and orange tones. In this family: Rosy Peach 2089-20; Santa Fe Pottery 1287; Peach Cobbler 2169-40; Orange Creamsickle 059; Fruited Plains 029; Navajo Red 2171-10; Spanish Red 1301; Adobe Orange 2171-30; Nautilus Shell 064; Morrocan Spice AF-285; Salsa Dancing AF-280; Rustique AF-275.

RED-ORANGES include intense shades of mango and cantaloupe. They include Orange Froth 151; Fruity Cocktail 147; Tangelo 2017-30; Tangy Orange 2014-30; Orange Burst 2015-20; Festive Orange, 2014-10; Orange Juice 2017-10; Peach Sorbet 2015-40.

PALE ORANGES are often described in fruity terms, such as peach and apricot. These colors impart a healthy glow to the skin, making them popular in baths and bedrooms. They include Marmalade 2016-40; Peach Crisp 159; Tangerine Zing 132; Orange Sherbet 122; Delicate Peach 120; Juno Peach 087; Melon Popsicle 2016-50; Cancun Sand 2016-70; Georgia On My Mind 134.

WARM ORANGE-YELLOWS are as cheery as an egg fried sunny-side up and range from marigold to sunflower. Colors in this family: Lemon Shine 2020-20; Nacho Cheese 2018-40; Sunflower 2019-30; Mandarin Orange 2018-20; Aura 169; American Cheese 2019-40.

GOLDEN YELLOWS have warm, brownish tones like those in honey and amber. Colors in this family: Showtime 293; Glen Ridge Gold 301; Goldfield 292; Golden Lab 178; Precious Ivory 185; Hawthorne Yellow HC-4; Morning Light 183; Halifax Cream 344; Candlelit Dinner 295.

BRIGHT, PURE YELLOWS are very powerful, luminous colors that draw attention to themselves. Colors include Yellow 2022-10; Yellow Rain Coat 2020-40; Lemon 2021-20; Sun Porch 2023-30; Sunburst 2023-40; Delightful Yellow 335.

BUTTERY YELLOWS are less powerful than pure yellows but have a warm, glowing quality. Colors in this family: Wildflowers 325; Good Morning Sunshine 326; Amarillo 320; Pale Moon 289; Butter 2023-60; Yellow Lotus 2021-50; Soleil AF-330.

GREENISH YELLOWS range from intense, citrus-flavored accents to muted, almost neutral mustards. Colors include Bright Gold 371; Citrus Burst 364; Mustard Field 377; Calla Lily 283; Treasure Trove 285; Yellow Roses 353; St Elmo's Fire 362; Mulholland Yellow 369; Citronee 281; Falling Star 351.

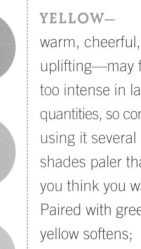

YELLOW— warm, cheerful, uplifting—may feel too intense in large quantities, so consider using it several shades paler than you think you want. Paired with green, yellow softens; paired with blue or violet, it brightens. Pale yellows give the illusion of day-light in light-deprived spaces. Intense orange can be a difficult color to live with; consider softer shades of apricot, peach, and mango.

inspirations

The rooms on the following pages, from leading designers and decorative artists across the country, demonstrate the tremendous variety of effects that can be achieved using the basic building blocks of paint, glaze, and a few simple tools: Consider the intricate Moorish stenciling of a romantic California hideaway, the jazzy, freeform mural in a contemporary kitchen, or the formal faux marble floor in an elegant entry. What truly lifts these rooms out of the ordinary is paint mixed with pure imagination. If you're a seasoned professional, there may be a technique or effect you've never seen used in quite this way before. And if you've never lifted a paintbrush, you may well be inspired to give it a try.

OPPOSITE
Not all decorative painting requires great skill or expertise. Vibrant multicolored stripes infuse this contemporary all-white living room with a burst of energy.
WALL COLOR: Skyscraper 765
STRIPES: Sparkling Sun 2020-30, Rockies Brown 2107-30, Little Piggy 2008-60, Key Lime 2031-50, Exotic Fucshia 2074-50, Red Tulip 2000-30

THIS PAGE
Oversized horizontal stripes
in two intense Chinese reds
immediately add drama and
personality to this plain wall.
Pairing colors that are close
in tone keeps the stripes from
becoming too assertive or
overwhelming.
STRIPES: Ryan Red 1314,
Geranium 1307

OPPOSITE
Combining the overscaled
brown-and-white geometry of
this floor treatment with the
traditionally styled reproduction
furnishings takes courage,
yet the result is a surprisingly
fresh, contemporary feel.
Executed by decorative painter
Jennie Schueler, the room is a
three-dimensional illustration
of how strong line and color
can tie together even the most
disparate pieces and give
them a modern twist.
COLORS:
Branchport Brown HC-72,
White

THIS PAGE

The Los Angeles home of a well-known music executive was conceived of as a Moorish fantasy, complete with Middle Eastern furnishings and stylized stenciling. Designer Martyn Lawrence-Bullard transformed this ordinary window alcove into an exotic oasis with a fabric-tented ceiling and an intricate stenciled border, inspired by traditional Ottoman designs. The chest is Syrian; the antique mirror is inlaid with camel bone.

OPPOSITE

Rather than hang art on the walls, New York architect and designer Craig Nealy chose to make the walls into art. Inspired by midcentury Guatemalan painter Carlos Merida, Nealy transformed his bedroom into a series of abstract geometric murals, in a unified palette of taupe, platinum, ecru, and pale orange. Decorative painter Eva Buchmuller executed the work from Nealy's sketches. The teak and ebony chest is a vintage Harvey Probber design; the bust is French, from the late 1940s.

COLORS:

Putnam Ivory HC-39,
Monterey White HC-27
Wickham Gray HC-171

OPPOSITE
Designer Samuel Botero felt that any interior featuring a Louis XVI settee and a two-thousand-year-old Buddha needed a decorative finish of equal weight and gravitas. He had Alpha Workshops paint the entry hall of this Manhattan apartment to simulate old stone construction; the effect was created by stamping out stone "blocks" with gesso and then applying multiple layers of glaze in a combination of warm and cool grays and taupes.

THIS PAGE
A warm, earthy palette of plum, greens, and browns grounds the soaring spaces of this Manhattan loft. The large expanse of wall, originally painted a chalky white, cried out for a more visually arresting decorative finish. The solution devised by Princeton interior designer Katie Eastridge: Venetian plaster applied over a base coat of soft gray, executed by Louise Crandell of Serpentine Studio. The iconic midcentury table is by Paul Frankel; the vase is twentieth-century mouth-blown Venetian glass.
BASE: Ashley Gray HC-87
COLUMNS: Hasbrouck Brown HC-71

THIS PAGE

The standard order of materials is reversed in this elegant Long Island home by the late Mark Hampton—the textile is on the walls and the paint is on the floor. An elaborate pattern of faux marble circles and squares lends the entry hall a formal weight, balanced by the striped upholstered walls.

OPPOSITE

For the elaborate faux marble treatment in this New York apartment, designer Jamie Drake took inspiration from a seventeenth-century specimen marble table in the room. Nick Hardy of Tallents Hardy painted the central panels Roman onyx and finished the frames and wainscoting to reproduce the look of rare marbles from Brescia and other Italian quarries.

OPPOSITE

The creators of this dramatic wall graphic, June Eng and Patricio Paez of IMURI Design, began with a digital image, which they projected onto the wall and painted free-hand. The black-on-brown effect has surprising impact: In strong light, the shadow flowers seem to take on a third dimension.

WALL: Van Buren Brown HC-70
FLOWERS: Black

THIS PAGE

San Francisco designer Jay Jeffers relied on strong color to create faux architectural detail in his California living room. By painting a band of warm buff on the white wainscoting and bordering it in a rich ribbon of brown fabric, he instantly added a three-dimensional element to the room.

WALL: Persimmon 2088-40
BAND: Pittsfield Buff HC-24

OPPOSITE

In a home rich with Indian accents, this intricate stenciled border both emphasizes the deep window seat and ties it seamlessly to the rest of the room. The decorative detail mirrors the elaborate carving and exotic colors of the fabrics and furnishings.

THIS PAGE

Designer Mark Christofi worked with mural painter Matt Cote to arrive at this fresh, inventive look for his own living room. The bold pattern on the wall is intentionally split almost evenly between positive and negative images, to keep the eye guessing as to the dominant color. The skull and crossbones chair is upholstered with antique funeral curtains; the organic shape of the coral lamp is a natural foil for the graphic wall design.

WALL: Super White Durango 2137-30

OPPOSITE

This winsome boy's bedroom in a historic Virginia farmhouse owes much of its appeal to the charming squirrel-and-bird stenciling. Adapted by designer Katie Ridder from a vintage Arts and Crafts wallpaper by British architect C. F. A. Voysey, the detail was enlarged to highlight the child-friendly woodland creatures. It was painted by the Willem Racké Studio in San Francisco.

WALL: Harvest Time 186

THIS PAGE

The subtle, feathery stenciling in this California dining room by John Turck of San Francisco's Turck-Nugent Design Studio gives the room an elegant, retro appeal. The warm, predominantly two-toned color scheme, with its silvery gray-and-taupe stencil over a lower wall of blue, keeps the room calm despite the abundance of pattern on the walls and rug. A pair of large silver torchères completes the vintage feel.

WALL: Wandering Heart 264
STENCIL: Silver 20

OPPOSITE

California interior designer James Lumsden turned to the color of Chinese famille rose china for the deep, delectable pink of his dining room. Decorative painter Matthew Menger applied layers of paint to the walls using both stippling and color-washing techniques. The result is a richly hued and textured background for his collection of Spanish Colonial art and eighteenth-century Mexican folk art angels.

BASE: Wild Heart 1354

GLAZES: Cranberry Ice 1362, Melrose Pink 1363

THIS PAGE

This playful pink child's room designed by Steven Miller Design Studio in San Francisco uses delicate painted detail to create a faux-formal French effect. Both walls and ceiling are enveloped in the same rosy shade, with white decorative touches, such as raised moldings and garlands, painted freehand on the walls. The cameo pillows on the trundle bed are custom-made.

BASE: Sweet 16 Pink 2002-60

MOLDINGS: Floral White OC-29

OPPOSITE
For these pale blue polished Venetian plaster walls, interior designer Lynn Morgan and decorative painter Shelly Denning were inspired by the aquatic colors of the David Hockney pool lithograph that hangs over the mantel. The soft sheen gives off a watery glow, while the warm tones of the wooden Swedish table and natural rattan chairs offset the cool, summery shade and give this Connecticut dining room almost a Caribbean feel.
WALL: Summer Shower 2135-60

THIS PAGE
Wood-graining techniques are usually thought of as a way to reproduce or enhance the natural tones and patterns of hardwoods. But in this romantic Tiffany-blue bedroom, designer Martha Angus shows how specialty tools and techniques can be twisted toward unexpected ends. The striated, wavy pattern on the walls and ceiling was created by Katherine Jacobus using a handheld graining heel, a tool more commonly used to imitate a crotch-grained effect on wood. The ornate gilded bed is a Venetian antique.
BASE: Billowy Down 2064-70
GLAZE: Costa Rica Blue 2064-50

THIS PAGE

Details pulled from traditional American decorative motifs cover the walls of this guest bedroom in a Long Island home. Designers Diamond and Baratta commissioned decorative painter Adam Lowenbein to create stylized versions of familiar Pennsylvania Dutch themes.

WALL: Glacier White OC-37
STENCIL: Buxton Blue HC-149

OPPOSITE

Decorative painters David Cohn and David Anderson used handcut stencils to reproduce silhouettes of traditional weathervanes on the floor of this Diamond and Baratta-designed kitchen. Stylized compass points helped tie the pattern together.

COLORS: San Francisco Bay 802
STENCIL: Yarmouth Blue HC-150

Zambian-born lifestyle guru Colin Cowie designed the mural for the kitchen of his Manhattan loft, telling his decorative painter, Michael Beneville, that he wanted something that looked like "a first-rate mural for a second-rate airline." The eye-catching result depends on a skillful layering of grays, blacks, and whites, taped off in an intricate grid and then painted freehand.

THIS PAGE
Treating the entire wall of this New York home as a canvas, June Eng and Patricio Paez of IMURI Design created brown and gold scroll details to complement the curving lines of the furniture.
SCROLLS: Van Buren Brown HC-70, Gold 10

3

glazing

The term "glazing" covers a multitude of techniques, ranging from soft, atmospheric color washes to more formal striés and stipple effects. In all of them, a glaze—a clear liquid medium to which color is added—is applied over a base color and manipulated with a brush, comb, rag, or other tool. As a result, the glaze and base colors are juxtaposed rather than mixed; it is the eye that blends them, creating subtle finishes of great depth and interest. (The nineteenth-century Impressionists and Pointillist painters called this "broken color.")

In positive, or applied, techniques such as color washing, glaze is added to the surface; in negative, or subtractive, techniques such as combing, glaze is selectively removed.

OPPOSITE
The rich apricot-glazed walls of architect Gil Schafer's New York apartment are given depth and texture with a crosshatched strié technique, done by Weidl Associates. The glowing color makes a flattering contrast to the sculptural black scagliola mantel, created by hand through a painstaking process of mixing color with plaster, then laying in colored threads to simulate marble veins.
BASE: Soft Beige 2156-60
GLAZE: Jack O'lantern 2156-30

glazing essentials

tips

- If you're applying a glazing technique with a partner, resist the temptation to switch roles halfway across a wall. Each person has a slightly different touch, and changes in style can sometimes make the whole wall appear "off."

- Since glaze is thinner than paint, it covers more surface area. Typically, a gallon of paint will cover about 400 to 450 square feet; a gallon of glaze will cover 500 to 600 square feet, depending on the technique. Use disposable plastic cups to measure your glaze recipe ingredients so you can easily mix up more, if necessary.

- Store glaze mixture in a sealed container between painting sessions. When you finish the job, save a small amount of the leftover glaze for touch-ups. Be sure to label and date the container.

Latex paints dry fairly quickly—an advantage when you're applying a base coat or doing stenciling, but a challenge with glazing techniques, when it's vital to have a long "open time" during which the paint stays wet enough to be manipulated. Adding a glaze extender to the glaze mix will lengthen that open time; but you will also need to work over small areas at a time with a partner, one applying the glaze and one manipulating it, to ensure that the glaze stays workable and that you keep a "wet edge" at all times. By their nature, most glazing techniques tend to be messy, so work on opposite walls protecting adjacent surfaces from splatters with extra taping, and latex gloves are a must.

PAINTS

Satin or semi-gloss paint is generally recommended as the base coat for decorative paint finishes—both create a surface that allows the glaze to glide over it without being absorbed and to be easily manipulated. Most of the techniques in this chapter were created using semi-gloss latex paint as a base coat.

GLAZES

A glaze is a translucent mix of commercially bought glazing liquid—essentially a paint with no pigment—mixed with a coloring agent, such as interior paint, artist's acrylic paint, or universal tint (see page 160). (The term *glaze* should not be confused with *top coat* or *varnish coat,* which are sealers meant to protect and/or provide sheen.) Glazes usually dry to a matte or at most eggshell finish; if you want a higher sheen—for marbling or wood graining, for example—apply a

gloss varnish coat once the glaze is dry.

In most cases, a latex glaze consists of four parts glazing liquid to one part paint, but you should experiment on sample boards to arrive at the best mix for a given technique. Adding more glazing liquid (or glaze extender) will increase the glaze's translucence.

GLAZE EXTENDERS

Compared to oil glaze, latex glaze is easy to use and environmentally friendly. But for techniques that rely on manipulating the finish, its faster drying time can be a challenge. The remedy is glaze extender—a colorless additive that is used to lengthen the open time, or working time, before the glaze starts to get too dry to be manipulated. Just a small amount of extender will keep the glaze wet and workable for a longer time period. This is especially useful in a time-intensive design, such as the combed basket-weave pattern on page 72, that requires precise, hands-on manipulation in a short time.

The extender should be added in small amounts; the amount needed depends on many factors: the air temperature and humidity, the texture and porosity of the base coat, the speed at which you work, and the complexity of the technique. Add just enough extender to give you the desired open time without sacrificing color, opacity, or transparency.

KEEP A "WET EDGE"

It's impossible to strié or rag a large area in a single pass—even with the help of an extender, some of the glaze will be too dry by the time you come to it. The solution is to work with a partner in small sections at a time so the glaze remains "open," or wet. One person rolls on the glaze, and the second person quickly manipulates it, proceeding from top to bottom and left to right in 2- to 4-foot-wide sections. When you work this way, you must keep a "wet edge": The person manipulating the glaze should stop about 4 inches from the leading edge of the fresh glaze, and the second person should roll on the next section of glaze so that it overlaps this edge by no more than ½ inch. Then the glaze can be manipulated across the "seam" to hide where the two sections meet. If the leading edge of the glaze begins to dry out, a line between the sections will become visible.

WORK ON OPPOSITE WALLS

When you work with glazes using bulky sponges or rags near an inside corner or ceiling, some glaze is likely to end up on the adjacent surface. The solution, for many glazing techniques and for

work with Venetian plaster, is to follow a slightly different work sequence: Mask off adjacent surfaces and complete opposite walls first, when those walls dry, mask them off and finish the remaining walls.

SAMPLE BOARDS

When you're eager to get started, it's tempting to dive right in without making a sample. But decorative techniques, especially glazing, take practice—even professionals create sample boards to guide their work.

Paint each sample on a 2-foot by 2-foot piece of drywall, rigid poster board, or foam board. (Avoid painting sample colors and glazes directly on the wall—you'll have to reprime the surface to hide the sample.) Two square feet is large enough to give you a good color sample as well as a feel for working the technique. Do all the steps you will do on the actual project: Prime first, apply two coats of the base color, then work with the glaze.

When the sample is dry, take it into the room you'll be painting and view it at different times of the day; give yourself at least a day or two to decide if you like it.

CHECKING YOUR WORK

If you're absorbed in detailed decorative work, face to the wall and brush in hand, it's hard to gauge the overall effect. Put down your tools and stand back, particularly early on in the job, to gain perspective on how work is proceeding. If you do this self-check often, you may be able to catch and correct aspects you don't like—a pattern that's looking too regular or too dense, a hole in your spatter technique, a glaze that needs thinning.

tips

- Be careful of overworking the corners of a room. Glaze tends to build up in corners, leaving a dark or ragged area in an otherwise uniform finish. Use a light touch to minimize the effect. If you're ragging or sponging, use a small piece of material in corners and other tight areas.

- Short winter days can be very limiting, especially if you're working on a subtle technique. Use halogen spot lights to let you continue work into the evening hours and provide extra light on overcast days.

- Organize the job so you have enough time to complete a full step or an entire wall before breaking for lunch or for the night. Never stop a decorative glazing technique in the middle of a wall. After you complete one wall, work the opposite wall next, to avoid damage to areas that are not fully dry.

mottling

Mottling—sometimes known as sponging—is one of the easiest and quickest finishes to execute. In its simplest form, where the glaze is applied, it requires just one person, though it may require more than one layer to achieve a finished look; mottling off, where the glaze is removed, is best done by two people: one to roll on the glaze, the other to manipulate it while it is still wet. For the best results, keep the base and glaze colors close in value; too great a contrast and the pattern can start to appear coarse. Experiment, too, with different sponges: Natural sea sponges create a random flowing pattern; synthetic ones tend to make more uniform marks.

MOTTLING ON WITH A SEA SPONGE

1 **MASK ALL WALLS** adjacent to where you'll be working with blue or green low-tack painter's tape. Prime the walls if necessary, apply two coats of satin or semi-gloss base color, and let dry for approximately 8 hours or overnight.

2 **PREPARE THE GLAZE** by thoroughly mixing 4 parts glaze and 1 part paint (in the glaze color) in a bucket. Mix in glaze extender as needed (see page 62). Pour a small amount of the mixture into a paint tray.

3 **DAMPEN A SEA SPONGE** with water to soften it, and squeeze the excess liquid out. Dip the flat side of the sponge into the glaze, then blot away excess glaze on an artist's paper palette. Holding the sponge lightly as you would a cotton ball, pounce the glaze onto the wall; turn the sponge slightly in different directions to avoid repetitive marks. Generally, the more densely applied the marks, the better the effect. Strive for a random but evenly applied lacy texture.

4 **TO WORK IN CORNERS,** use a small wedge cut from the sponge, or dip an artist's brush into the paint and dab into the inside angle to mimic the mottled effect.

5 **IF YOU'RE WORKING** alone, step back and view the wall from time to time to make sure the application is even. On large surfaces, a second person can follow behind you, filling in uneven areas. If there are areas where the pattern seems too "solid," or if you want to soften the overall look, try sponging back in with a glaze of the base color after the glaze has dried.

LEVEL
Beginner
(passionate novice)

NUMBER OF PEOPLE
1 or 2

SPECIALTY TOOLS
• Several sea sponges of varying shapes and pore sizes
• Artist's paper palette for blotting

APPLICATION METHOD
See page 154.

PREPARATION
As you would for any painting project, prepare the surface and mask off the ceiling, baseboards, doors, and window trim.

OPPOSITE
BASE: Decorators White
GLAZE: Manchester Tan HC-81

tips

- Don't worry if the glaze drips—you can pounce off drips as you work. This is why it's best to work from top to bottom—never start at the bottom.

- Step back from the wall at regular intervals and view the work to make sure that you're applying an even finish. If you wait until you've finished an entire wall, the glaze will be too dry to fix.

THIS PAGE
BASE: Smoldering Red 2007-10
GLAZE: Eggplant 1379

stippling

Soft and delicate, stippling—dabbing and removing small amounts of glaze with a dry brush or cheesecloth—creates a subtle, timeworn look. Professionals generally use a stipple brush to achieve a perfectly even result, but nonprofessionals are better off using cheesecloth; it produces a more relaxed look, allowing for imperfections, and tends to be easier to handle than a brush.

STIPPLING WITH CHEESECLOTH

1 **MASK ALL WALLS** adjacent to where you'll be working with blue or green low-tack painter's tape. Prime the walls if necessary, apply two coats of satin or semi-gloss base color, and let dry for approximately 8 hours or overnight.

2 **PREPARE THE GLAZE** by thoroughly mixing 4 parts glaze and 1 part paint (in the glaze color) in a bucket. Mix in glaze extender as needed (see page 62). Pour a small amount of the mixture into a paint tray.

3 **WORK IN 3-FOOT-WIDE** sections. Cut the glaze into corners and along the edges with a foam roller or 2½-inch angled trim brush. With a roller, apply the glaze from the top of the wall to the bottom.

4 **HOLD A PIECE** of bunched-up cheese-cloth so there is one smooth working surface. Starting in the top corner and working your way across and down, pounce the cloth onto the wet glaze, removing the glaze and leaving a very fine suedelike pattern. Work to about 4 inches from the wet edge (see page 63).

5 **CONTINUE THE POUNCING** motion over the 3-foot-wide section of wet glaze, from ceiling to baseboard. Rearrange the cheese-cloth as it becomes loaded with glaze. When it starts to put on more than it is removing, discard the cheeesecloth for a new piece.

6 **ROLL ON THE NEXT** section of glaze, overlapping the wet edge by about ½ inch without disturbing the previously completed area.

LEVEL
Expert
(trained and experienced)

NUMBER OF PEOPLE
2

SPECIALTY TOOLS
- Cheesecloth, cut into approximately 2-foot squares
- Foam roller or short (³⁄₁₆-in.) nap roller

APPLICATION METHOD
See page 155.

PREPARATION
As you would for any painting project, prepare the surface and mask off the ceiling, baseboards, doors, and window trim.

tips

• The lighter your touch with the rag on the wall, the more delicate the pattern. The more absorbent the rag, the more glaze you'll remove, revealing more base coat color. Before choosing a rag to remove the glaze, experiment on sample boards until you find the effect you're looking for.

• Try not to rinse your rag in the middle of a wall as this will create a light spot next to an already glazed area.

THIS PAGE
BASE: Organdy 1248
GLAZE: Pink Paradise 003

ragging

Ragging can produce a range of effects, from a subtle and indistinct pattern to a strong textured look, depending mainly on the relationship between the base color paint and the glaze (the closer in value, the more subtle the result). Like mottling, ragging is deceptively simple: Although it's quick and simple to execute, it can easily look crude or heavy-handed, so it pays to practice on sample boards to get a look you like.

RAGGING OFF

1 MASK ALL WALLS adjacent to where you'll be working with blue or green low-tack painter's tape. Prime the walls if necessary, apply two coats of satin or semi-gloss base color, and let dry for approximately 8 hours or overnight.

2 PREPARE THE GLAZE by thoroughly mixing 4 parts glaze and 1 part paint (in the glaze color) in a bucket. Mix in glaze extender as needed (see page 62). Pour a small amount of the mixture into a paint tray.

3 WORK IN 3-FOOT-WIDE sections. Cut the glaze into corners and along the edges with a foam brush or 2½-inch angled trim brush. With a roller, apply a thin coat of glaze from the top of the wall to the bottom.

4 SLIGHTLY DAMPEN a rag with water to soften it, then bunch it loosely in your hand. Lightly pounce the wet glaze just enough to lift it. Stay a few inches shy of the wet edge (see page 63). Keep rearranging the rag in your hand to prevent repetitive marks.

5 ROLL ON THE NEXT 3-foot wide section of glaze, overlapping the wet edge by about ½ inch without disturbing the previously completed portion.

6 TO CONTINUE THE effect in corners and tight spaces, bunch up a small rag and dab gently into the angles.

LEVEL
Intermediate
(patient and talented)

NUMBER OF PEOPLE
2

SPECIALTY TOOLS
• Several rags, about 2 feet square, to create the pattern

APPLICATION METHOD
See page 154.

PREPARATION
As you would for any painting project, prepare the surface and mask off the ceiling, baseboards, doors, and window trim.

color washing

This is one of the easier techniques—a freeform finish that involves simply brushing paint diluted with water and glaze over a base color. The subtle watercolor effect is most impressive: soft, yet with depth and texture, and very forgiving on less than perfect walls. The instructions below call for using a brush, but you could equally use a sponge to "wash" the walls with color. Although this is an applied technique, it's a good idea to work with a partner, one person working across the wall and the other painting in the edges around the ceiling and base.

COLOR WASHING WITH A BRUSH

1 **MASK ALL WALLS** adjacent to where you'll be working with blue or green low-tack painter's tape. Prime the walls if necessary, apply two coats of satin or semi-gloss base color, and let dry for approximately 8 hours or overnight.

2 **PREPARE THE GLAZE** by thoroughly mixing 3 parts glaze and 1 part water and 1 part paint (in the glaze color) in a bucket. Mix in glaze extender as needed (see page 62). Pour a small amount of the mixture into a paint tray.

3 **WITH A GLAZING BRUSH**, whisk the glaze across the wall with random crisscross motions, overlapping brushstrokes. Work quickly, using the brush to catch any drips. Alternatively, you can dip a cloth or sponge into the glaze mixture, then apply using a random circular wiping motion, as if you are washing the wall.

4 **FOR A MORE** saturated, even effect, apply a second coat of the glaze in the same random fashion after the first coat has dried. The end result should be evenly balanced translucent veils of color.

LEVEL
Beginner
(passionate novice)

NUMBER OF PEOPLE
1 or 2

SPECIALTY TOOLS
• 4-inch-wide glazing brush with soft bristles

APPLICATION METHOD
See page 152.

PREPARATION
As you would for any painting project, prepare the surface and mask off the ceiling, baseboards, doors, and window trim.

OPPOSITE
BASE: Decorators White
GLAZE: Cape Blue 1642

tips

• For one-of-a-kind designs, make your own combing tool by cutting teeth into a rubber-edged window squeegee. Or cut a plastic lid in half, then cut teeth into the straight side.

THIS PAGE
BASE: Cork 2153-40
GLAZE: Gettysburgh Gold 1064

Depending on how it's manipulated, a triangular-shaped rubber painter's comb can create a variety of patterns, ranging from simple lines to undulating moiré patterns that resemble fine silk (see page 79). In this pattern, the glaze is applied in three-foot-square sections then combed in three-inch squares in alternating horizontal and vertical directions. The effect resembles coarsely woven cloth. Because the squares within each section are the same size as the comb, no taping is needed.

CHECKERBOARD WALL

1 **MASK ALL WALLS** adjacent to where you'll be working with blue or green low-tack painter's tape. Prime the walls if necessary, apply two coats of satin or semi-gloss base color, and let dry for 8 hours or overnight.

2 **USING A RULER** and a level, measure and lightly mark in pencil horizontal lines every 3-inches across the wall.

3 **PREPARE THE GLAZE** by throughly mixing 4 parts glaze and 1 part paint (in the glaze color) in a bucket. Mix in glaze extender as needed (see page 62). Pour a small amount of the mixture into a paint tray.

4 **CUT THE GLAZE** into corners and along the edges with a foam brush or 2½-inch angled trim brush. Roll the glaze on in 3-foot-square sections at a time. Work carefully—try to minimize any overlap between sections.

5 **STARTING AT THE TOP** left corner of the rolled-on glaze, drag the comb down to the first line. Repeat on the next row starting 3-inches in. Continue in the same way down the 3-foot area, alternating the starting point, and then work across, spacing each vertical section 3-inches apart until the area is covered.

6 **IMMEDIATELY COMB** the remaining squares horizontally in the 3-foot section of glaze to complete the checkerboard effect.

7 **ROLL ON THE NEXT** 3-foot-square section of glaze and repeat Steps 5 and 6, alternately combing vertical squares then horizontal squares until you have completed the wall.

LEVEL
Expert
(trained and experienced)

NUMBER OF PEOPLE
1 or 2 (for a larger area)

SPECIALTY TOOLS
- 3-inch triangular-shaped comb with small rubber teeth
- T square or other right-angle tool
- Level
- Tape measure
- Pencils and erasers
- Metal ruler

APPLICATION METHOD
See page 153.

PREPARATION
As you would for any painting project, prepare the surface and mask off the ceiling, baseboards, doors, and window trim.

Strié, in which a glaze color is dragged off in long strokes with a dry brush or other tool, creates a silky-looking finish, elegant and somewhat formal. The technique—an essential one in wood graining as well—takes practice and a nimble and steady hand to achieve the long, unbroken lines that mark this look. On walls, the key is to work in small sections and in pairs, one person dragging from the top, the other from the bottom, so the lines are smooth and the glaze is manipulated before it dries.

STRIÉ WITH A HARD-BRISTLE BRUSH

1 MASK ALL WALLS adjacent to where you'll be working with blue or green low-tack painter's tape. Prime the walls if necessary, apply two coats of satin or semi-gloss base color, and let dry for approximately 8 hours or overnight.

2 PREPARE THE GLAZE coat by thoroughly mixing 4 parts glaze and 1 part paint (in the glaze color) in a bucket. Mix in glaze extender as needed (see page 62). Pour a small amount of the mixture into a paint tray.

3 WORK IN 3-FOOT-WIDE sections. Cut the glaze into corners and along the edges with a foam brush or 2½-inch angled trim brush. With a roller, apply a thin coat of glaze from the top of the wall to the bottom.

4 PULL A HARD-BRISTLE brush with the bristles facing up and slightly angled toward the wall about three quarters of the way

down the wall. Do not lift the brush from the surface. The glaze coat should be dragged immediately so it doesn't become too stiff to manipulate.

5 WHILE YOU ARE pulling down, have your partner drag up from the baseboard to meet and overlap your brushstrokes; this will eliminate stops and starts in the dragged lines. After each drag, wipe the brushes with a clean rag to prevent a buildup of glaze. To help keep your lines straight, attach a plumb line to the ceiling a few feet ahead of the wet edge (see page 63).

6 REPEAT ACROSS THE 3-foot-wide section, stopping a few inches short of the wet edge. Roll on the next 3-foot section of glaze, overlapping the wet edge by about ½ inch without disturbing the previously completed portion.

LEVEL
Intermediate
(patient and talented)

NUMBER OF PEOPLE
2

SPECIALTY TOOLS
- Two 4-inch-wide hard-bristle brushes
- Plumb line

APPLICATION METHOD
See page 153.

PREPARATION
As you would for any painting project, prepare the surface and mask off the ceiling, baseboards, doors, and window trim.

OPPOSITE
BASE: Iguana Green 2028-10
GLAZE: Avocado 2145-10

variations

1 PARCHMENT SQUARES
For this soft and subtle look from Alpha Workshops, first tape out a grid on the wall. Adjust the size of your squares so they divide equally into the space (the squares here are 16 inches). With a stipple brush, stipple the taped-off squares with the first glaze in a random manner; let dry. Stipple a small brushful of the second glaze into the corners of each square so that the darker corners fade to lighter centers. Let dry. Repeat the process on the remaining squares.
BASE: Linen White
GLAZE 1: Greenfield Pumpkin HC-40
GLAZE 2: Jamesboro Gold HC-88

2 STRIÉ CROSS-HATCHING
Combining a horizontal and vertical strié creates a grass cloth or linen look. Working in 3-foot sections,drag a hard-bristle brush vertically through the glaze. Allow to dry overnight, then drag through a second coat of the glaze horizontally.
BASE: Passion Fruit 2171-40
GLAZE: Umbria Red 1316

3 STEEL WOOL STRIÉ
For a coarser strié, use 000 steel wool and drag through a very thin coat of glaze. Use a plumb line to help keep the lines straight. Wipe the steel wool clean regularly and replace when saturated.
BASE: White
GLAZE: Dusk to Dawn 1446

1 PARCHMENT SQUARES

2 STRIÉ CROSS-HATCHING

3 STEEL WOOL STRIÉ

4 FADEAWAY STIPPLING

5 TWO-GLAZE COLOR WASH

4 FADEAWAY STIPPLING

Roll the darker glaze (1) onto the bottom third of the wall, then stipple with cheesecloth from the bottom up. About halfway up, apply a band of the lighter glaze (2) and stipple upward, blending to achieve a gradual fade. At the top, rather than blending, you're removing glaze to reveal as much of the light base color as possible. This requires a lot of manipulating and blending, so use extender to keep the glazes wet.

BASE: Peace and Happiness 1380

GLAZE 1: Purple Rain 1386

GLAZE 2: Carolina Plum 1384

5 TWO-GLAZE COLOR WASH

Pour a small amount of each glaze into separate paint trays. With a 4-inch brush, dip into the first glaze, then off-load onto an artist's paper palette, leaving a small amount on the brush. Gently whisk over the wall in large figure-8 patterns until it is covered. Let dry. With another brush, repeat with the second glaze (visible as hints of orange/umber), working lightly and weaving the colors together to soften the overall look.

BASE: Pink Lace 2081-60

GLAZE 1: Wild Pink 2080-40

GLAZE 2: Butterscotch 2157-30

variations

1 STRIÉ STRIPES
This summery effect from Alpha Workshops is a very simple combination of two techniques: strié and taped stripes. Tape off the areas to be striéd, then apply the glaze rather heavily and strié with a hard-bristle brush so the glaze doesn't "melt" back into the base coat. Let dry. Tape off 1-inch stripes on either side of each striéd section and paint.
BASE: Linen White
STRIÉ STRIPE: Yellow Highlighter 2021-40
SOLID STRIPE: Summer Blue 2067-50

2 MOIRÉ COMBING
To create a dazzling moiré effect, drag a rubber comb tool horizontally through a 3-foot section of glaze in straight lines. Then, immediately drag the comb over the same area, again horizontally but this time moving the comb in an undulating motion. Continue in 3-foot sections across the wall.
BASE: White
GLAZE: Brazilian Blue 817

3 STRIPED COLOR WASH
Roll on two coats of the base color, allow to dry. Using a large brush apply the glaze in random strokes over a 3-foot wide area, then immediately apply the second glaze and blend while both are wet. Allow to dry. Apply the third glaze in the same random fashion to soften the effect; let dry. Mark off and tape the stripes (ours are alternating ¼-inch and

1 STRIÉ STRIPES

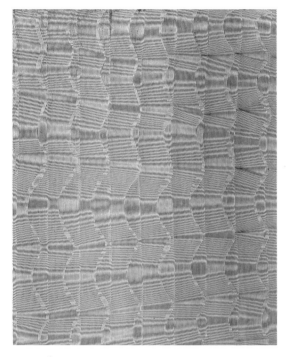

2 MOIRÉ COMBING

3 STRIPED COLOR WASH

4 TWO-COLOR STIPPLE

5 PLASTIC RAGGING

1-inch wide). Roll on the stripe color, then remove the tape.

BASE: Woodmont Cream 204
GLAZE 1: Coastal Fog 976
GLAZE 2: Brandon Beige 977
GLAZE 3: Leap of Faith 210
STRIPES:: Stuart Gold HC-10

4 TWO-COLOR STIPPLE

Roll on the first glaze, then pounce the surface with the stipple brush to lift the glaze and allow some base color to show through, resulting in a fairly uniform surface. Wipe the glaze off the brush each time you pounce. Let dry. Repeat with the second glaze color.

BASE: Dusky Blue 1640
GLAZE 1: Sonoma Skies 737
GLAZE 2: San Jose Blue 741

5 PLASTIC RAGGING

Plastic wrap can be manipulated on wet glaze in various ways. A piece stretched tightly creates a random linear pattern much like the veining in marble; a large piece, rumpled and held loosely like a rag, will leave a sharper-edged pattern than cotton fabric will. Work in 3-foot-wide sections, as you would for ragging off (see page 69). If you find that the pattern is too strong, repeat the process, rolling from side to side across the wall. Because plastic isn't absorbent, you'll need to replace it often when it becomes too wet with glaze.

BASE: Angel's Wings 1423
GLAZE: Queen's Wreath 1426

variations

1 PLAYFUL WOOD GRAIN
Alpha Workshops used a
bright color to contribute a
contemporary edge to traditional graining. To begin, the
base color was applied with a
cellulose sponge. The glaze
was rolled on in small sections
so it would remain workable
while first a rubber comb then
a graining heel were drawn
vertically through it to simulate
the natural striations of wood.
BASE: Hibiscus 2027-50
GLAZE: Eccentric Lime
2027-30

**2 BASKET-WEAVE
COMBING**
For this woven pattern of
straight and wavy lines, start
by dragging a triangular-
shaped comb straight down
through the glaze. Repeat this
motion, leaving approximately
a 1-inch band between the
vertical stripes. Working in
3-foot sections, comb short,
wavy lines horizontally through
the vertical bands, skipping
every other stripe. Continue
staggering the horizontal wavy
lines. (Each wavy band will
start and stop on the 1-inch
uncombed stripe.)
BASE: White
GLAZE: Cedar Green 2034-40

3 RAG ROLLING
To create a dreamy driftlike
pattern effect, fold and roll a
damp, clean rag about 18
inches square into a sausage
shape, then slightly twist the
center. Holding the roll at both
ends, gently roll it vertically

1 PLAYFUL WOOD GRAIN

2 BASKET-WEAVE COMBING

3 RAG ROLLING

4 BLUE COLOR WASH

5 STIPPLED CHECKERBOARD

down a 3-foot-wide section that has been coated with glaze; the rag roll will pick up the glaze, leaving a repetitive pattern. Varying the tightness of the roll will achieve different looks.

BASE: Pearl River 871

GLAZE: Iced Slate 2130-60

4 BLUE COLOR WASH
Starting at the top of the wall, apply the lighter glaze (1) with a chip brush in side-to-side motions in horizontal bands. Introduce a small amount of the darker glaze (2) about a quarter of the way down, blending it into the lighter glaze to make a subtle transition. Gradually add more of the darker glaze in intervals as you move down the wall. While the glaze is still wet, blend the colors from top to bottom to soften all transitions.

BASE: Heavenly Peace 746

GLAZE 1: Bainbridge Blue 749

GLAZE 2: Blue Toile 748

5 STIPPLED CHECKERBOARD
After you've completed the cheesecloth stippling technique on page 67 (with the first glaze), measure and mark your pattern. Tape off alternating squares to protect them. Working on one untaped square at a time, apply the second glaze with a sponge brush or roller, then stipple off.

BASE: Mill Springs Blue HC-137

GLAZE 1: Turquoise Mist 695

GLAZE 2: Pale Avocado 2146-40

on location: artful elegance

THIS CLASSIC GEORGIAN HOME sits amid nine acres of manicured gardens, its redbrick halls dominating a sculpted landscape that includes a formal parterre, plus a fountain, stonework, and statuary. Built in the 1940s, when skilled crafts-manship was flourishing, the original design was expanded in recent years to include a new wing, making the house perfectly symmetrical.

Such stately architecture cries out for formal, elegant treatment. Yet "formal," in this house, doesn't translate into stiff or austere. Instead, the large, light-filled rooms are infused with warmth and color. The living and dining rooms both face south, with generous windows capturing an abundance of sun and garden views. High ceilings and classical proportions give the spaces a serene, spacious air, and the owner's extensive array of antiques and china nestle naturally into the dignified setting.

The two rooms also house an important collection of twentieth-century art, and it was those paintings that interior designer Isabelle Vanneck first looked to when choosing the unexpectedly deep, vivacious shades and finishes that grace the walls. "When you have very fine paintings and furniture, the colors should enhance those assets, rather than distract from them," she explains.

In the dining room, for example, walls are done in a rosy crosshatched glaze, echoing the burnished wood tones of the antique English table and Queen Anne chairs and picking up the background colors in a painting in the room. The base color is a creamy ivory; the pinkish glaze coat is dragged and woven in a broad plaid effect—a pattern bold enough to create some geometric interest, yet disciplined enough to blend gracefully with the composed surroundings. The warm color deepens and glows in lamp or candlelight, making it an excellent choice in a formal dining room often used at night.

The living room, painted by Lisa and Stephen Longworth, is done in an airy turquoise strié. The subtle lines of the glaze coat, which bear a strong resemblance to raw silk, are echoed in long silk curtains in the same shade of blue. The crisp texture provides a handsome frame for the room's imposing art, while the soft sheen of the glaze lends the walls a luminous quality.

"A flat painted wall would have been boring and dull next to all this fabulous art, and wallpaper would have been distracting," says Vanneck. "It needed rich, textured color that could pick up the tones of the art and furniture and complement them. And that's exactly what we created."

stenciling
and stamping

4

The pineapple and fruit basket designs of colonial America may be the first examples that come to mind, but figurative and abstract stencil and stamped patterns can be found in almost every every age and every culture. The Egyptians, Greeks, and Romans all made extensive use of stencils decoratively while in Japan highly intricate stencils for kimonos reached their peak over five hundred years ago.

It's not hard to understand the appeal of stenciling: The tools could hardly be more straightforward—designs can be cut from everyday materials—and a simple repeat pattern can be created quickly and without a lot of skill.

In this Manhattan apartment designed by Samuel Botero, the tone-on-tone oversize damask stenciling by Alpha Workshops was further softened by multiple glaze coats. The result is a design that seems almost suspended in a mist of hazy color. The vase is a Picasso.

stenciling essentials

MYLAR

Mylar is a semitransparent film used for graphic arts and is the preferred material for stencil making. (Stencil plastic can also be used, but it's a bit more difficult to cut.) It is sold by the sheet and in rolls at art supply stores and is available in several thicknesses. Look for Mylar that's shiny on one side and frosted on the other side, 5 millimeters thick.

Before picking up a stencil brush, it's always advisable to draw your design to scale on graph paper; that way you can determine the best spacing and allow for any awkward breaks caused by windows or doors or the like.

A commercially bought precut stencil is fine for most purposes, especially if you're a beginner and want to start with something uncomplicated. But when you truly want a custom design—one scaled to fit a particular space or to match a fabric pattern in the room, for example—you can cut your own stencil. For multicolor designs, you'll need several stencils, one for each color; including registration marks on each will enable you to align them properly.

PLANNING A LAYOUT

Stencils play a number of decorative roles. A stenciled border can substitute for a crown molding or chair rail, raise the eye in a room, or provide interest on a plain wall. Border designs can also run vertically, to accent doors and windows or to create the look of wallpaper.

To plan the layout of your design, measure the area you intend to stencil and draw it to scale on graph paper. A scale of 1 inch = 1 foot works well; to draft large spaces, use a scale of $\frac{1}{2}$ inch = 1 foot. Measure the stencil motif and decide on a space between motifs, then calculate how many you can comfortably fit across the wall or floor. Don't be afraid to finesse the spacing a bit in awkward or tight spots; a little quirky spacing will add whimsy and charm to the design.

Before starting, do some tests on scrap paper to get the right paint consistency and to practice the brush motion (see page 157). An aggressive swirling movement will make the filled color more opaque, while an up-and-down pouncing motion will create a lighter, more shaded look. The following are tips for specific layouts.

REPEAT MOTIFS Executing a repeat pattern with large, widely spaced stencil motifs requires careful measuring. Small, closely spaced patterns tend to be more forgiving. The larger the pattern or repeat width, the more noticeable any breaks will appear. Your goal with such allover "wallpaper" patterns is for the designs to finish at the corners in a pleasing way. One option is to start the design in the center of the space and work outward toward the corners, adjusting the spacing slightly as you get closer to the corners so the pattern doesn't break awkwardly at the edge of the wall. Alternatively, you can divide the area into a grid of rectangles or squares, then center a motif into each section or into alternating sections (for a staggered pattern).

If you have difficulty visualizing the right spacing, stencil some samples on newspaper (or make photocopies) and tape them to the wall or floor to try out different spacing possibilities. Once you have the spacing worked out, transfer the design to scale onto graph paper; this allows you to see how the complete design will look. Then, using a snap line and measuring tape, mark the corresponding positions on the wall or floor lightly, in pencil or chalk.

BORDERS To position a stenciled border, measure down from the ceiling (or out from the molding, window, or baseboard) and use a snap line to create a guide. Confirm the placement with a plumb line, level, or ruler. If you're using Mylar or plastic, mark the edges of the border on the face of the stencil with two strips of tape.

If you're designing a border, such as a vine or geometric pattern, you'll have to find a way to change direction at corners without an awkward break in the pattern; a simple miter at the corner is sometimes not sufficient. Many commercially available border stencils include an extra design element specifically designed for filling out or turning corners.

MAKING A STENCIL

Begin by sketching or tracing your design, full size, on tracing paper or transparent graph paper. If you plan to use more than one color, key in the colors. This drawing will be your reference when you cut the stencils (one for each color) and when you apply the colors.

Cut a piece of Mylar at least 2 inches larger all around than your design. Place the sheet, frosted side up, on top of your drawing and trace the design onto it with a sharp pencil. Use a metal ruler or straightedge to draft straight lines. To smooth out curves, use a French curve (available at art supply stores) or trace around saucers or other round household objects.

CUTTING Place the Mylar, marked side up, on a cutting mat or a thick piece of plate glass. Cut on the marked lines with an X-acto knife held at a 45-degree angle. To help maintain a smooth edge, keep the knife blade stationary and rotate the film. Cut out smaller areas first to avoid weakening the stencil. Use a metal ruler or straightedge to cut straight lines.

MULTICOLOR DESIGNS One-color designs are painted from a single stencil, but multicolor designs require a separate one for each color because each is painted individually. Registration marks ensure that all the colors stay aligned.

Cut one piece of Mylar for each color, 2 inches larger all around than your design. To make registration marks, hold all the sheets together with the edges aligned and use a hole punch to make holes at all four corners. Center one sheet, frosted side up, on top of the drawing, then insert a pencil through the registration marks and mark their positions on the drawing. Trace the shapes for *one color only* onto the Mylar. Remove the Mylar and set it aside. Place a second sheet of Mylar on the drawing, align the registration marks with the pencil marks on the drawing, and draw the shapes that use the second color only. Repeat this process until you have a separate stencil for each color. Cut out the stencils with an X-acto knife and label them so that you know which color to use with each

tips

• Try to cut several copies of your stencil—you'll have a replacement should the original get damaged or worn out, and when paint builds up on the one you're using, you can switch to a clean one.

• It's quite easy to position some abstract stencil patterns incorrectly—for example, placing them upside down or flopping them left to right—especially once paint begins to build up on them. To avoid mistakes, attach a small piece of painter's tape or masking tape on your stencil to indicate the top and front of the design.

stenciling essentials

tips

- To stencil a ceiling, try using a temporary spray adhesive on the back of the stencil instead of tape. (Choose a product with low VOCs.) This option is suitable for all surfaces except newly painted ones, where the finish might pull up. Always test a temporary adhesive product in an inconspicuous place on the stenciling surface and follow the manufacturer's directions. Respray when the adhesive begins to lose its tack.

- To clean stencils of accumulated paint, soak them in water in a flat disposable baking pan. After the paint has loosened, gently remove it with a sponge and wipe dry.

This Connecticut hallway shows how the use of an intricate stencil in a tone-on-tone color scheme creates a very sophisticated look.
COLORS: Navajo White, Bennington Gray HC-82

one. Some stencilers use a fine-tip permanent marker to mark key features of the overall design on each stencil; while not a substitute for registration marks, these lines can aid the registration of the different colors during the stenciling process.

HOW TO STENCIL

Set the stencil in position and tape it in place at the corners. If the stencil will butt up against the ceiling or an adjacent wall at a corner, protect these surfaces with wide blue or green low-tack painter's tape.

If you're stenciling a border, start at the midpoint of the border and work out to the edges. This way it is easier to finesse the spacing as you near the corners to make a corner stencil fit.

APPLYING THE PAINT Dip the tips of the stencil brush into the paint, then swirl it on an artist's paper palette to off-load any excess; the brush should be nearly dry.

Hold the brush perpendicular to the surface and swirl firmly in the stencil opening. Use your free hand to hold down the edges of the stencil. Be careful not to overwork any particular area; as soon as the color appears, move on. Reload the brush as needed, offloading the excess paint on the palette before applying it to the stencil.

Carefully peel up the tape and lift the stencil straight up—don't slide or shift it or the paint will smear. Turn the stencil over and wipe off any paint seepage on the reverse side with a dry cloth. Place it in the next position (consult your plan), tape the edges, and repeat the process. Continue in this fashion, incorporating any special

corner designs as you come to them, until the entire design is complete.

MULTIPLE COLORS Begin with the most prominent color in the design. Tape its stencil in position and lightly mark the four registration dots on the wall or floor with a pencil. Apply the color, move the stencil to the next position, and repeat. Continue in this way until the entire area has been stenciled in the first color.

Begin the second color when the first color is dry to the touch. Set the appropriate stencil over the previous work, and align the registration dots. Apply the second color. Move the stencil to the next position, and repeat. Continue until all the colors are painted. Let the paint dry completely, then carefully erase all the penciled registration marks.

FINISHING Well-designed stencils rely on a system of narrow links, called bridges, to connect the cutout areas. Without bridges, some of the cutout shapes in the stencil might be so large or awkward that the stencil would become too flimsy to stand up to rigorous brushing. While bridges facilitate the stenciling process, they don't have to show in your final work. Once you've stenciled a design on the wall or floor, you can always go back over the work with a small artist's brush to fill in the areas that were masked by the bridges.

tips

• To line up the stencil pattern consistently across the room, mark a chalk grid with a snap line on the floor. This is especially important for aligning asymmetrical designs.

There is a variety of clear coatings to protect a floor stencil. Water-borne (acrylic) versions are easier to work with, have less odor than alkyds, and will not yellow over time. Whether you choose acrylic or alkyd, do a test beforehand on a sample board to make sure the stencil pattern does not bleed or lose clarity. Apply once the stencil pattern is fully dry, following the manufacturer's directions.

STENCIL: Georgian Brick
HC-50

Almost any simple pattern or shape can be adapted to a stencil design, then the size and layout customized to suit the space in which it is to be used. The brocade pattern below is a wonderful way to dress up a wooden floor. The design—laid out here in a drop brick, or staggered, pattern—complements the pickled floorboards in an entrance hall and shows how effective a simple one-color stencil can be.

BROCADE FLOOR

1 **DRAW A PLAN** of the floor to scale on graph paper. Include entryways, staircases, and other architectural elements.

2 **SELECT A POINT** on which to center the design; most often this will be the middle of the room, but it could also be a doorway or other architectural feature. Keeping in mind that the spacing of the pattern should work with the size of the stencil and the scale of the room, sketch out the rest of the pattern on graph paper; this will give you an opportunity to adjust for awkward breaks around the edges of the room.

3 **USING A METAL RULER** and a snap line, transfer the plan to the floor and mark the position of each stencil pattern lightly in pencil.

4 **STARTING AT THE CENTER** point of the design, secure the stencil to the floor with blue or green low-tack painter's tape.

5 **LOAD THE STENCIL** brush with a small amount of paint and work the paint into the bristles in a circular motion on an artist's paper palette. Apply the paint to the stencil; use as little as possible to avoid seepage underneath. Lift a corner to see if the application is as opaque as you'd like; apply a second coat if necessary.

6 **WORK OUTWARD** from the first stencil, stenciling individual motifs until one row is completed. Wipe the stencil with a clean rag from time to time. Continue until the floor is completed.

7 **LET THE PAINT DRY** overnight (at least 12 hours), then apply an acrylic polyurethane coating following the manufacturer's directions.

LEVEL
Intermediate
(patient and talented)

NUMBER OF PEOPLE:
1 or 2 (if using a snap line)

SPECIALTY TOOLS
- Precut one-part stencil, purchased or made yourself (see page 000)
- Stencil brush(es) or foam roller (size depends on size of design) and paint tray
- Small artist's brushes for touch-up and details

APPLICATION METHOD
See page 157.

PREPARATION
If necessary, sand the floor and prepare it to accept paint, following manufacturer's directions. Mask off the baseboards and trim. Paint or stain as desired.

border patterns

Drawing your own stencil is the ultimate in custom design; this delightful three-part wall border was designed by a young artist—with a little help from his mother. Because each color has its own separate stencil, it's essential to add registration marks so they can all be properly aligned.

FISH PARADE

1 **USE A SNAP LINE** to mark the top and bottom of the border on the wall. Tape the outside of the edges of the border with blue or green low-tack painter's tape. With a foam roller, roll on the background color of the border. Allow to dry.

2 **WITH A SHARP PENCIL,** sketch or trace the border design to the desired size on tracing paper.

3 **CUT 3 PIECES OF MYLAR** at least 2 inches larger all around than your stencil design. Mark the edges of the border on each piece of Mylar with pieces of tape and use a hole punch to create registration marks following the instructions on page 87.

4 **MARK EACH MYLAR** sheet for one of the colors and trace the relevant part of the design with a sharp pencil on the frosted side. Place each sheet on the cutting mat and cut out with an X-acto knife (see page 87).

5 **PLACE THE FISH** stencil on the border at the midpoint of the wall. Align the tape registration marks with the edges of the border and lightly mark the four registration marks on the wall with a pencil.

6 **LOAD THE STENCIL** brush with a small amount of paint and work the paint into the bristles on an artist's paper palette in a circular motion. Apply the paint to the stencil; use as little as possible to avoid seepage underneath. Lift a corner to see if the application is as opaque as you'd like; apply a second coat if necessary. Remove the stencil and reposition it within the border. Continue in this manner until you have painted the first color around the entire border. Allow to dry.

7 **GO BACK TO WHERE** you started stenciling and position the second stencil. Align the registration marks and stencil in the second color all around the room. Let dry. Repeat with the third stencil.

LEVEL
Intermediate
(patient and talented)

NUMBER OF PEOPLE
1

SPECIALTY TOOLS
- Stencil brush(es) or foam roller (size depends on size of design) and paint tray
- Mylar sheet, one side frosted and the other side clear
- X-acto knife and extra blades

APPLICATION METHOD
See page 157.

PREPARATION
As you would for any painting project, prepare the surface and mask off the ceiling, baseboards, doors, and window trim.

BACKGROUND: Tropicana Cabana 2048-50
FISH: Douglas Fir 2028-20, Rolling Hill Green 2047-30, Poolside Blue 2048-40
GRASS AND BUBBLES: Shore House Green 2047-50
WATER: Ocean Spray 2047-60

tips

• Before starting, test your stamp on newspaper to determine the right amount of paint to use. Too much will cause drips and may cause the stamp to slide and smear; too little and the pattern will be too light.

• Step back regularly as you work and look at the pattern to make sure the density is consistent.

• Mist the stamp with water from time to time, then blot it on newspaper, to remove excess paint and keep the surface from drying out.

BASE: Orleans Violet 1374
GLAZE: Caribbean Sunset 1377
FLOWERS: Lazy Afternoon 1378

stamping

Whereas stencils lend themselves to intricate, lacy patterns, stamped designs are better suited to less complex shapes, their straightforward shapes and varying colors only adding to their charm. Both ready-made and custom-designed stamps of all kinds can be purchased at art supply stores or online; or you can cut your own design from a piece of dense foam rubber. Here, a soft color wash provides an atmospheric background for a lighthearted floral pattern.

FLOWER STAMP

1 **SKETCH OR TRACE** your design at actual size on paper. Use double-sided tape to tape the paper to a foam rubber sheet, then cut around the design with an X-acto knife or sharp scissors. Remove the paper and tape.

2 **GLUE THE FOAM**-rubber design to a wood block slightly larger than your design using white household glue.

3 **COLOR-WASH** the wall (follow the color washing step-by-step instructions on page 71). Let dry.

4 **DRAW THE PATTERN** to scale on graph paper so you can see the overall design. Mark the desired spacing lightly on the wall in pencil. If you need help visualizing the design, experiment first by stamping it on newspaper and taping it to the wall.

5 **POUR A SMALL** amount of paint into a shallow plastic container or onto an artist's paper palette. Pick up a thin, even layer of paint on a foam roller, then roll the paint on the stamp.

6 **PRESS THE STAMP** firmly on the wall, then remove it; be careful not to smear it sideways. For sharp impressions, roll a new thin film of paint onto the stamp each time you use it.

LEVEL
Beginner
(passionate novice)

NUMBER OF PEOPLE
1

SPECIALTY TOOLS
- Foam rubber sheet, at least $\frac{1}{2}$ inch thick
- Wood block the size of your stamp or slightly larger, about 1 inch thick
- X-acto knife and extra blades
- Small foam roller (the size of your stamp)

PREPARATION
As you would for any painting project, prepare the surface and mask off the ceiling, baseboards, doors, and window trim.

variations

1 GOLD STAMPING

This stamped pattern by Alpha Workshops is about as simple as you can get: Score a raw potato several times vertically and horizontally in a crosshatch pattern. Lightly pat the paint onto the potato stamp with a chip brush, then apply to the wall (the pattern here was roughly spaced by eye). Using a dark background color enhances the drama of metallic paint.

BASE: Chelsea Gray HC-168
STAMP: Gold 10

2 CIRCLE WALL PATTERN

Roll on the base coat; this should always be the lightest color. The stencil is in two parts: the oval shapes that make up the circles and the diamond centers. Spray-mount the ovals stencil and apply to the wall, then roll on the darkest color. Let dry and remove. Now position the second stencil in the center of the circles you've just created. Roll on the last color.

BACKGROUND: Golden Archway 146
CIRCLES: Oriole 2169-30
DIAMONDS: Vegetable Patch 062

3 FLOWER STENCIL

This playful asymmetrical design works well as an overall pattern or centered on a wall as a piece of "art" in itself. Here, two highly saturated colors give it a "pop" look.

BASE: Scandinavian Blue 2068-30
STENCIL: Grape Green 2027-40

1 GOLD STAMPING

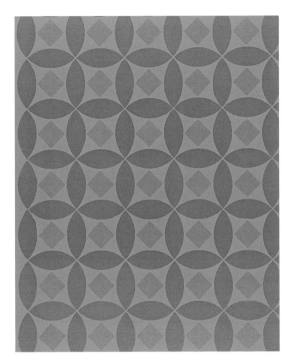

2 CIRCLE WALL PATTERN

3 FLOWER STENCIL

4 GREEK KEY BORDER

5 STAGGERED SQUARES

4 GREEK KEY BORDER

For the background, use a sea sponge to mottle on the three-colors in succession. Spray-mount one side of your stencil and apply it to the wall. Roll on the gold glaze color; use two coats to give the design a more saturated, prominent look. Remove the stencil, and touch up with an artist's brush if necessary. Repeat across the entire wall.

COLORS: Toronto Blue 2060-40,
Seaside Blue 2054-50,
Tear Drop 2060-70
STENCIL: Gold 10

5 STAGGERED SQUARES

This look is achieved with one stencil. Roll on two coats of the base color. Spray-mount the stencil, apply it to the wall, and roll on the first color. Let dry. Position the same stencil a bit lower and to the right of the first, apply the second color. The aim is to create a shadow-like pattern, however you don't need to be precise in the placement.

BASE: Crème Fraiche 2023-70
STENCIL 1: Sundance 2022-50
STENCIL 2: Bright Yellow 2022-30

variations

1 BAMBOO FOREST

Like many stamped patterns, the charm is in its imperfections—the "holidays" in the paint that give the pattern a handmade quality. Alpha Workshops made a large stamp, 20 inches by 15 inches wide, from ordinary blue foam insulation. It was applied across the wall; in some places the blocks overlap, in others they don't quite meet—the key is to not create a perfectly repeating pattern. You can use a plumb line to keep you from veering too far off course vertically, but there's no need to draw guidelines on the wall. Keep in mind that it takes some stamina to print a whole wall with a block this size.
BASE: Grizzly Bear Brown 2111-20
STAMP: Silver 20

2 BUTTERFLY BORDER

To create this flirty wall border, use two different butterfly stamps. Roll on two coats of the base color. Put the stamp color on an artist's paper palette or paint tray, then roll it onto the first stamp and press onto the border. Repeat, alternating the stamps.
BASE: Beachcomber 993
STAMPS: Spring Sky 674

3 MONOGRAM GRID

Something as simple as this stamp made from a monogram can serve to make an intriguing pattern or border.
BASE: Pear Green 2028-40
STAMP: White

1 BAMBOO FOREST

2 BUTTERFLY BORDER

3 MONOGRAM GRID

4 FLOATING GINGKO LEAVES

5 WHITE DIAMONDS

4 FLOATING GINGKO LEAVES

These floating, scattered leaves make a design virtue out of the randomness possible with stamped patterns. Either purchase a stamp or draw and cut your own leaf shape using a real leaf as a template. Work one color at a time, overlapping some of the leaves to suggest a three-dimensional effect.

BASE: Norfolk Cream 261
LEAVES: Freedom Trail 277, Caribbean Cool 661, Jalapeno Pepper 2147-30

5 WHITE DIAMONDS

Roll on two coats of the base color. Slap a flogger on an artists' paper palette holding the first glaze so that it is distributed evenly on the brush. Wipe off excess with a rag. Flog the wall vertically and horizontally covering it with a random overall pattern. Spray-mount one side of the stencil and apply it in a staggered pattern; you can position it by eye for a more informal look. Roll the white glaze over the stencil and dab it off with cheesecloth to create this transparent effect.

BASE: Juneau Spring 2041-40
GLAZE: Majestic Blue 2051-40
STENCIL: (glaze): Dove Wing OC-18

variations

1 FLOATING ACANTHUS
Roll on two coats of the base color. With a chip brush, dry-brush on the white glaze, blending overall into the wall; let dry. Spray-mount the stencil and position it on the wall in a random manner, as if the leaves were windblown. With a stencil brush, fill in the stencil with a circular motion, letting the base color show through in places to give an aged look. Remove the stencil. Use an artist's brush to highlight some areas of the leaves and create a three-dimensional feeling.
BASE: Perfect Peach 2167-50
GLAZE: Linen White
STENCIL: Soft umber glaze (within stencil)
HIGHLIGHT: Linen White

2 DAMASK WALL PATTERN
This overall damask pattern uses a precut one-part stencil. Because of its size it may need two people to apply it to the wall. Roll on the base color, then spray one side of the stencil with adhesive and apply to the wall. Roll on the glaze and lightly dab cheese-cloth to give an aged look.
BASE: Pearl River 871
STENCIL: Stone Harbor 2111-50

1 FLOATING ACANTHUS

2 DAMASK WALL PATTERN

3 FLORAL WALL BORDER

4 AGED BORDER

5 LUMINOUS FLOWERS

3 FLORAL PATTERN

This Japanese-inspired one-part stencil is painted in two colors and could be adapted to run around a room as a border. Roll on two coats of the base color, spray one side of the stencil with adhesive and apply to the wall. Apply the flower color with a stencil brush then fill-in the diamonds using a small stencil brush.

BASE: Clearspring Green HC-128
FLOWERS: Douglas Fern 563
DIAMONDS: Summer Nights 777

4 AGED BORDER

This faded background is produced by dry brushing and selectively removing color. Roll on two coats of the base color. Pick up a small amount of the glaze on a chip brush; wipe off excess on a rag. Dry-brush in a cross-hatch pattern. Allow to dry. Spray-mount the stencil on one side and apply to the wall. Roll the gold paint over the stencil, then quickly dab off small amounts to create an aged effect.

BASE: Peale Green HC-121
GLAZE: Sea Glass PT-330
STENCIL: Bryant Gold HC-7

5 LUMINOUS FLOWERS

The subtle, shimmering qualities of pearlescent glazes are enhanced when paired with a flat color in an overall tone-on-tone pattern.

BASE: Decorators White
GLAZE: Stillness PT-390

on location: turkish delight

THIS SUBTLY EXOTIC New England home is the product of an international mix of sensibilities: the understated British tastes of its owners, interpreted by the sophisticated eye of interior designer Sara Bengur, daughter of a Turkish economist who spent much of her childhood in Istanbul. Bengur's cosmopolitan aesthetic is rich with Eastern influences: the peaked, Moorish shape of a window treatment; the love of pattern, which shows up in the antique textiles she brings back from her travels; the custom-designed stencils she favors.

In this house, the walls in the large, light-filled living room are covered in a sinuous, leafy stencil pattern, which was created by picking out a detail from an ancient Egyptian frieze and enlarging it to nearly life-size. The painted vines, executed by Dean C. Barger, wind their way from floorboards to ceiling, echoing the natural shapes of the trees outside the windows and the play of light during the day. The repeating, vertical thrust of the pattern and subtle coloration—a light taupe for the stems and pale blue dots for the fruits and flowers, highlighted against a washed-out terra cotta—allow the design to recede into the background while still giving the walls depth and tactile interest.

"The client wanted things simple, and although these are elaborate patterns, the effect is discreet—just very light and airy and fanciful," says Bengur. "It's a matter of scale and color. I look for patterns everywhere—historic references, books, textiles, rugs, architectural features I notice on the street. Then I change the detailing and play with the scale and color and placement until it feels right."

Stenciling can also set up a beautiful interplay with the patterns in textiles and other furnishings. In the living room, the lithe tendrils on the walls are repeated in the supple shapes of an iron table leg and the floral embroidery on a daybed cushion. In an upstairs guest bedroom, a simple, Moroccan-inspired stenciled border echoes the lacy pattern in an antique bedside screen. The pale blue of the border picks up the colors in the upholstered headboard and bedding, and the continuous geometric motif acts as a visual drawstring, pulling in the walls and ceiling of a large space and giving it a cozier feel.

"Decorative painting always adds to the individuality of the room," says Bengur. "With wallpaper, someone could walk in and say, 'Oh, I've seen that at a friend's house.' But when you create a stencil, you really personalize a room and make it your own. It's completely unique."

THIS PAGE
The guest bedroom is a lovely collection of low-key lacy patterns, from the stenciled border to the intricate screen to the antique textiles used in the decorative pillows.
WALL: Decorators White
STENCIL: Icy Blue 2057-70

OPPOSITE
The stencils in the living room add a whiff of exoticism and visual intrigue, but the subdued color scheme keeps it discreet enough to avoid dominating the space or competing with art and furnishings. The inviting daybed is one of a pair Bengur had custom-made for the house.
WALL: Antique White
STENCIL: Dark Beige 2165-40, Monroe Bisque HC-26, Atrium White

geometrics 5

While checkerboard floors, stripes, and other geometric designs in this chapter work in traditional settings with restrained colors or tone on tone, these are also the paint techniques to turn to when you want to add a modern graphic flair to your decor. Taped patterns can be striking and bold, with a definite nod to the clean lines of contemporary design, and the colors can be as bright and playful as your imagination will allow. In general, geometrics aren't hard to paint, but they do call for careful and patient planning, measuring, and taping. Even the simplest stripes will be more professional looking with some advance consideration about dealing with corners, doors, and other architectural elements.

The star and stripes of this Connecticut farmhouse floor by Michael Stanley make a powerful graphic impact and give a contemporary twist to a traditional entry hall.
COLORS: White, Balboa Mist OC-27, Black

measuring and taping essentials

SNAP LINES

Use a chalk snap line to quickly and accurately mark longer guidelines on walls and floors. (Make sure you get one that uses *chalk*—some snap lines leave indelible marks.) With a partner, stretch the line between your two measured points. Pull the string taut, then snap it against the wall or floor. The string leaves a chalk line that you can follow for taping. Wipe off any leftover chalk with a damp rag or dry brush before painting.

TAPE

Blue or green low-tack painter's tape comes in assorted widths ranging from ³⁄₄ inch to 3 inches. For quicker, more economical taping, try to plan your design to make use of exact tape widths whenever possible.

OPPOSITE

The clear, luminous color and regular geometry of faux stone blocks by decorative painter James Barry give this small study by Mark Hampton an air of serene elegance. The classical furnishings contribute to the feeling of a monument in miniature.

Geometric effects, such as blocks, stripes, and checkerboard patterns, owe much of their success to careful measuring and taping. The first step is to work out the right scale and proportions for the design on graph paper. This more than repays itself: It makes measuring and taping much easier; enables you to adjust the scale of the pattern to suit the space; and, for more complex designs, helps you figure out the painting sequence. After that, the painting itself is often fairly quick.

BLOCKS AND BRICKS

A staggered block pattern, known as "drop brick," will create the look of laid stone or brickwork. Measuring and taping it is fairly easy, and painted grout or mortar lines will add realism and dimension for a trompe l'oeil effect. The smaller the grout line, the more delicate the look; the wider the line, the heavier and more solid the blocks will appear.

MEASURING AND DRAWING Measure the height and width of each wall to be painted and draw it to scale on graph paper. Include all architectural elements, such as doors and windows. A scale of 1 inch = 1 foot works well; to draft large spaces, use a scale of ½ inch = 1 foot.

Sketch your block design on the scale drawing, starting at the center and working out so that incomplete blocks fall at the edges. There's no set size for stone—the blocks can be any size and proportion you want. For a large room, try a block size of 18 inches by 14 inches; in a smaller space, try 16 inches by 12 inches.

Ideally, adjust the block height so it divides evenly into the wall height. If a partial row is unavoidable, run it along the baseboard, where it will be less noticeable. You might also try to adjust the block position and size to minimize awkward breaks around windows and doors, at the ceiling, and at outside and inside corners. There's no need to allow for grout lines in the plan—you'll be creating them in taping.

PAINTING THE BASE COLOR Apply two coats of the base color in a satin finish; this will show as grout lines in the finished work. If you plan to apply sand paint, Venetian plaster, or another textured finish on top, a flat base coat is preferable. Allow to dry following the manufacturer's recommendations.

MARKING AND TAPING To speed the layout of the pattern on the wall, cut an L-shaped template from a sturdy piece of cardboard so that the outer edges of the L match the height and width of the blocks.

OPPOSITE
The antique toile fabric on the slender side chair was the inspiration for the broad rose-and-white stripes in this East Hampton bath. Designer Zina Glazebrook worked with decorative painter Lori Barnaby to create the look.
STRIPES: Geranium 1307, White

Start marking at a top corner of the wall; refer to your plan for the position of the first block. Working from top to bottom, slide the template vertically down the wall and lightly mark the height of each block as you go. Mark the other edge of the wall the same way. Then, working with a partner, snap horizontal lines to connect the marks. Use a level to confirm that the lines are true.

Now begin marking individual blocks. Start at a top corner and slide the template across the wall, marking the width of each block lightly with pencil or chalk. Complete all the blocks in the top row. To create a drop brick pattern, in row 2 position the template half a block's width in from the edge, to stagger the rows. Mark this block, then continue along the row. Mark row 3 and all remaining odd-numbered rows the same as row 1. Mark row 4 and all remaining even rows the same as row 2. Follow your graph paper plan to mark any special sizes or shapes when you reach door or window openings.

To create the grout lines, center $3/4$-inch blue or green low-tack painter's tape or, for narrower lines, use graphic tape available at art supply stores, over the pencil block outlines. Burnish the edges of the tape with your finger. To achieve very thin grout lines—$1/8$ inch or less—mask around individual blocks.

STRIPES

Painting stripes is an easy way to create a custom look for a room. Vertical stripes can visually elongate a wall and make a ceiling look higher. Horizontal stripes make a room feel more spacious and can visually lower a high ceiling. Bear in mind that most rooms, especially in older houses, are not square and

stripes will tend to make that more visible. This problem will be less obvious with vertical stripes because the unevenness will fall in the corners. But horizontal stripes will highlight any dips or slopes in the ceiling.

For movement and interest, introduce stripes of varying widths in a mix of colors. You can also combine horizontal and vertical stripes to create a freestanding border design or to highlight a door or window. The pattern variations are endless, particularly when you introduce several different colors.

MEASURING AND DRAWING While stripes are relatively easy and quick to paint, they require careful planning, especially if multiple colors or widths are involved.

Measure the height and width of each wall you intend to paint and draw it to scale on graph paper. Include all architectural elements, such as doors and windows. A scale of 1 inch = 1 foot works well; to draft large spaces, use a scale of $1/2$ inch = 1 foot.

Sketch your design on the graph paper, starting at the center of the main wall and working out. Stripes are typically between 2 inches and 12 inches wide. Complete the design using colored pencils or markers to gauge the impact of your color scheme. Tone-on-tone stripes, such as beige and cream, will appear less busy than a high-contrast scheme such as black and white. Try to avoid glaring breaks in the pattern or color sequence at the corner edges and around doors and windows. Make all your adjustments on paper before starting to tape.

PAINTING THE BASE COLOR Apply two coats of the base coat color (the lightest color

measuring and taping essentials

BURNISHING
Burnishing the edges of the tape is essential for a tight seal. Special burnishing tools are sold at art supply stores, but you can also use a plastic credit card, single-edge razor blade, or your finger to smooth the tape. Just make sure the edges are sealed—it's time far better spent now than retouching areas where paint has seeped underneath.

OPPOSITE
Zina Glazebrook designed the painted floor in this Long Island summer home to lend a note of formality to a room that doubles as the main entry to the home.
FLOOR: Manchester Tan HC-81, Davenport Tan HC-76

you are using in the design); use a satin or high-sheen finish for the base color and the stripes if you're going to apply glaze later on. Allow the second coat 8 hours or overnight to dry before you start taping. Paint that hasn't cured fully will be pulled off when the tape is removed.

MARKING AND TAPING Begin taping on the focal wall of the room—the wall facing the main doorway or perhaps the longest wall. For vertical stripes, measure and mark a vertical line from ceiling to floor using a plumb line and center the first stripe on that line. Measure and lightly mark the remaining stripes across the wall with a snap line. Use a level or plumb line to confirm that these lines are perpendicular and parallel to each other. For horizontal stripes, snap the first line at the top of the wall, from edge to edge, and work down from there so that any partial stripes appear at the foot of the wall.

To ensure that you transfer the correct color sequence to the wall, label each stripe lightly with pencil or chalk to indicate its color, then compare your labeled work stripe by stripe against the graph paper plan—once you've put the tape up, it's easy to paint the wrong area, especially if your design uses three or more colors.

Paint stripes, one color at a time, in a light-to-dark sequence; making the base color one of the stripes. When masking, apply blue or green low-tack painter's tape along the outside edges of the stripes you're going to paint. Burnish the edges well to ensure a tight seal. Mark a light X in chalk or pencil on any exposed areas that you won't be painting at this time.

After you paint, wait just until the surface is dry to the touch before taking off the tape. If you wait too long to remove the tape, paint that seeped underneath may dry out and become difficult to remove and the tape may leave behind a sticky residue. Wipe away any seepage from under the taped area with a clean damp cloth; use a small brush for touch-ups, if needed.

Let the paint dry completely, or at least 24 hours, before taping off the stripes for the next color. Wipe off or erase any chalk or pencil marks in the new areas before you begin painting.

CHECKERBOARDS

Typically, a checkerboard pattern is rendered in two colors; squares that are the same color touch each other at the corners. Extreme precision is required when taping and painting to ensure a crisp, clean rendering of this geometric pattern. If you let the existing floor color be one of the colors in the design, you need to tape and paint only once.

After you've mastered the basics, you may want to attempt more complex designs, such as the floor shown opposite; this variation features small contrasting key tiles at the block intersections and is surrounded by a solid border (glimpsed to the left of the table).

MEASURING AND DRAWING Measure the length and width of the area and draw it to scale on graph paper. For a floor design, include all entrances, doors, and closets. For a wall design, include doors, windows, and other architectural elements. A scale of 1 inch = 1 foot works well; to draft large spaces, use a scale of $\frac{1}{2}$ inch = 1 foot.

Draw your checkerboard design on the scale drawing. Generally, a full checkerboard square, rather than a point of intersection, is more pleasing

measuring and taping essentials

OPPOSITE

tips

- Wait until the paint is completely dry before attempting to remove any pencil or chalk lines used to mark out the design. Use a soft rubber eraser; wipe off any remaining chalk lines with a damp cloth.

OPPOSITE
Patrizio Paes and June Eng of IMURI Design based this high-impact geometric treatment on a favorite plaid shirt, minus a few lines. The red wall with black-and-white accents is a study in powerful contrasts, bringing the large room down to human scale.
COLORS: Jeweled Peach 2013-30,
Black 2132-10,
White

at the center of the layout, but this isn't a hard-and-fast rule. The size of the squares can range from 6 inches to 18 inches, or even larger in big spaces; the scale depends on how busy you want the pattern to be. After you have mapped out the checkerboard grid, use colored pencils or markers to gauge the impact your color choices will have. Colors that are close in value or adjacent on the color wheel will subdue the pattern. For a crisp look, choose stark contrasts, such as black and white.

PAINTING THE BASE COLOR In an allover checkerboard design—one in which the grid pattern extends to the edges of the wall or floor—there are two color areas to consider. For a wall design, apply two coats of the base color, just as you would for a striped wall. For a floor, you can apply a base color if desired, or you can skip the base coat application and simply designate the existing floor color as the base color.

MARKING AND TAPING Start by marking the center of the floor or wall. Use a tape measure and a snap line (and a plumb line for walls) to snap the horizontal and vertical grid lines following your graph paper plan.

Decide which squares will be painted and mark an X with chalk or pencil on all the other squares. Apply blue or green low-tack painter's tape around the edges of each unmarked square. Trim the ends of the tape with an X-acto knife and straightedge, so they don't cross into the adjacent squares you're going to paint, pressing just hard enough to make a clean cut through the tape.

After painting, wait just until the surface

is dry to the touch before removing the tape. Wipe away any seepage from under the taped area with a clean cloth (be careful not to step on any freshly painted areas!). Use a small brush for touch-ups, if needed. Let the paint cure completely, at least 24 hours, before proceeding with any additional taping and painting (for example, to add key tiles, as shown on page 000). Be especially careful when cutting through or removing this tape to avoid marring the finish underneath. Wipe off or erase any chalk or pencil marks of any new areas before painting.

FINISHING FLOORS Make sure the paint or stain is thoroughly cured before applying a protective finish—overnight or, better still, 24 hours is a safe period of time to allow for drying. For most cases, an acrylic polyurethane, in either a low lustre or gloss finish, is the best choice. Alkyd polyurethanes tend to yellow slightly and are harder to clean up. Follow the manufacturer's instructions for application but before applying the coating over the whole area, check for compatibility by applying the coating to a sample board of the design to confirm it doesn't cause any bleeding or loss of clarity.

Inspired by traditional Chinese lattice designs, this panel could fill an entire wall or serve as an accent in an entryway. Use the measurements here as a guide only; you can alter the scale to suit your space. The actual painting is easy and quick; what takes the time is measuring and taping. Drawing the pattern to scale before starting is essential to clarify the steps involved.

CHINESE LATTICE PANEL

1 DRAW THE BACKGROUND panel on graph paper to scale. You can choose any dimensions you want for the design.

2 TO SCALE, DRAW HORIZONTAL lines on the graph paper from top to bottom of the panel the same distance apart as the height of each link. Starting one link width in along the second horizontal line, mark a full link width, then a space, and continue to mark link widths followed by the spaces along the line. Do the same along the last horizontal line drawn.

3 WITH A PENCIL, connect the marks vertically, skipping every other horizontal line. The result is a grid of alternating rows of rectangles, evenly separated.

4 CONNECT THE RECTANGLES vertically: Draw a line from the center of the bottom edge of one rectangle to the center of the top edge of the one below it, and so on down the length of the panel.

5 ERASE THE LINES between the rectangles to reveal the chain link design.

6 USING A SNAP LINE and ruler, mark the the dimensions of the panel on the wall; tape the perimeter with 1-inch blue or green low-tack painter's tape. Apply two coats of the link color. (To give the outline added weight, we taped a double border around the panel.) Allow to dry overnight. Leave the tape in place.

7 FOLLOWING THE SAME steps used to create the scale drawing, transfer the link pattern to the wall using a ruler and snap line. Center 1-inch-wide blue or green low-tack painter's tape on the chalk-link pattern.

8 PAINT TWO COATS of the main color over the entire panel. Allow to dry, then remove the tape to reveal the lighter-colored links. Erase any chalk marks with a damp cloth.

LEVEL
Intermediate
(patient and talented)

NUMBER OF PEOPLE
2

SPECIALTY TOOLS
- Snap line
- X-acto knife and extra blades
- $3/8$- by $1/2$- inch nap roller cover
- $3/4$-inch lamb's wool nap roller cover

PREPARATION
As you would for any painting project, prepare the surface and mask off the ceiling, baseboards, doors, and window trim.

OPPOSITE
MAIN COLOR: Clinton Brown HC-67
LINKS: Decatur Buff HC-38

checkerboard

This brown-and-white double checkerboard is derived from an eighteenth-century design but enlarged for a more contemporary feeling. If you think of it as two separate patterns—one of the large brown-and-white squares and a second one of opposite-colored, smaller squares within them—the steps involved in taping and painting become easier to visualize and execute.

DOUBLE-SQUARE FLOOR

1 **MEASURE AND MARK** a simple checkerboard pattern on the floor using a snap line or laser level. (We've chosen 3-foot squares.)

2 **STARTING IN THE MIDDLE** of the room, apply blue or green low-tack painter's tape to the outside edges of the center square. This square will become one of the large white squares; mark it lightly in chalk with a W in the center. Continue taping the outside edges of alternate squares and mark each with a W.

3 **PAINT EACH MARKED** square with two coats of white paint; follow the manufacturer's suggested drying time in between. (Erase the chalk marks before painting.) Allow to dry approximately 8 hours or overnight. Carefully remove the tape.

4 **TAPE AROUND** the outside edges of the remaining squares (this new tape will fall on the white squares) and paint with two coats of brown paint; follow the manufacturer's suggested drying time in between. Allow to dry.

5 **TAPE THE SMALLER** squares that are centered within the large ones. Our small squares are 2 feet in size, so they have a 6-inch border on all sides. Tape the outside edges. Repeat for the remaining squares.

6 **APPLY TWO COATS** of brown or white paint, as appropriate, to the small squares. Allow to dry overnight, then apply an acrylic polyurethane following the manufacturer's instructions.

LEVEL
Intermediate (patient and talented)

NUMBER OF PEOPLE
1 or 2

SPECIALTY TOOLS
- $\frac{3}{8}$- by $\frac{1}{2}$-inch nap roller cover
- $\frac{3}{4}$-inch nap roller cover

PREPARATION
Prepare the floor and paint with one coat of white primer following manufacturer's instructions. Allow to dry.

OPPOSITE
COLORS:
Branchport Brown HC-72, White

variations

1 FRESCO BORDER
Alpha Workshops used a flat cellulose sponge to apply the first glaze in a light circular motion; two coats create this cloudy, suedelike look. For the border, tape off the design, then paint it in with a stipple brush; hand paint the outline with a $\frac{1}{4}$-inch flat acrylic artist's brush. The second glaze coat, highly diluted with glazing liquid and applied lightly over the entire area, lends a weathered look and softens the contrast between the border and the the wall.
BASE: Linen White
GLAZE 1: Avocado 2145-10
KEY: Avocado 2145-10
KEY OUTLINE: Burnt Caramel 2167-10
GLAZE 2: Winding Vines 532

2 MULTICOLOR STRIPES
Begin with the lightest color; this will serve as the base and will be the color of one of the stripes. Tape off the stripes in the pattern you've chosen; mark lightly with a pencil to identify which colors go where. Paint one color at a time. Let dry, then remove the tape.
STRIPES:
White,
Dill Pickle 2147-40,
Pebble Creek 1453,
Comet 1628,
Mountain Laurel AC-20,
Iced Slate 2130-60

3 PINSTRIPES Roll on two coats of the base color (this becomes the stripes). Tape off $\frac{1}{4}$-inch stripes about 5 inches

1 FRESCO BORDER

2 MULTICOLOR STRIPES

3 PINSTRIPES

4 BLACK DIAMONDS

5 TWO COLOR LATTICE

apart. Roll on the first glaze then mottle on the second glaze with a sea sponge to create the look of aged leather.

BASE: Rhododendron 2079-50
GLAZE1: Wood Grain Brown 2109-30
GLAZE2: Saddle Soap 2110-30

4 BLACK DIAMONDS

Roll on two coats of the white base color. Tape off 3-inch stripes 4 inches apart; these will be the black stripes. With $\frac{1}{4}$-inch tape, tape off the diamond pattern within the 3-inch stripes. Roll on the black paint, then remove the tape. Now tape off a $\frac{1}{4}$-inch vertical border on both sides of each black stripe and paint with an artist's brush.

BASE: White Dove OC-17
STRIPES: Black 2132-10

5 TWO COLOR LATTICE

Adding a second color to a simple lattice or grid gives it an added sense of depth. Roll on two coats of the first lattice color. Using a snap line, mark and tape off the overlapping lattice pattern. Roll on two coats of the base color. Remove the tape, allow to dry, then tape off the X shape within each diamond (shown here in blue); paint in the second lattice color with a small brush.

BASE: Angel's Trumpet 278
LATTICE COLOR 1: White Dove OC-17
LATTICE COLOR 2: Airway 828

on location: house of a different stripe

PERCHED ON THE SEVENTEENTH FLOOR of a Miami Beach high-rise, this seaside apartment is a study in casual glamour. Sweeping ocean views fill the rooms with shimmering light, while the curvaceous floor plan and controlled color palette give it the feel of a perfect pearlescent seashell. Yet like so much new construction, the space began as a generic sheetrock box. The owners, a couple of transplanted New Yorkers, brought in Manhattan designer Miles Redd to personalize the rooms with a dose of 1940s-inspired modernist style, expansive enough to incorporate both French antiques and beachlike touches of sea grass and sisal. Redd and decorative painter Chris Pearson employed a variety of decorative paint techniques to enhance the physical space, from lacquered ceilings to broad horizontal striping on the walls to faux panels on the flat doors. The result is an alluring, light-as-air environment shaped by a sophisticated use of color and line.

In the living room, glowing, lacquered walls and ceiling the color of oyster bisque bring to mind the tactile, translucent interior of a conch shell—an effect bolstered by a white Flokati rug anchored by a midcentury table with a spiral, shell-like base.

To ground this soft, seductive space, Redd gave the doors a strict geometric treatment, with flat faux panels painted in shades of buff and ivory. The approach adds backbone to what would otherwise be a nondescript architectural feature and introduces a bit of discipline to the luxurious atmosphere. "We took a stock door, and with just a little paint, made it something special," says the designer.

The use of controlled line and pattern is taken even further in the study, where broad horizontal stripes of soft acqua and cream wrap around the walls. "Horizontal stripes have a 'mod' feel, which seemed appropriate in Miami, with all the Deco and modern architecture," says Redd. "Somehow vertical stripes feel like you're trying to do English country, which would be so out of place in this context." The

strong graphic element is the perfect foil to the sensuality of the other rooms, yet the carefully chosen colors, all of which share a yellow undertone, are close enough in nature that the stripes have punch without being overpowering. And since the room opens onto a sweep of terrace overlooking the water, the beachside palette of aqua, cream, and taupe links the space naturally to the view beyond.

"It's just a great example of using painterly techniques to transform a space," says Redd. "We've gone from a white builder's box to an urbane, soothing retreat."

THIS PAGE

In the study, the broad stripes are a witty nod to the meeting of white sand and sea outside the windows. The graphic effect keeps the room grounded in the midst of such expansive ocean views; the horizontal thrust is in keeping with the modernist spirit of the room and the urban setting of the apartment.
STRIPES: Antiguan Sky 2040-60,
Linen White

OPPOSITE

Painted with flat faux panels, plain builder's doors make a strong geometric statement. The boxy shape is a nice counterpoint to the striped study immediately adjacent, where the panel color is picked up on the wall.
DOORS: Shaker Beige HC-45
PANELS: Linen White

texture and special finishes

6

The luminous wax-rubbed finish known as Venetian plaster has been adorning Italian villas for hundreds of years. Today's store-bought Venetian plasters don't require as many coats as traditional mixes, and they can be produced in any color in a fan deck, but the application of several very thin, very smooth layers of skim coat still requires a great deal of skill and patience.

Metallic and pearlescent glazes are new finishes that offer a range of decorative possibilities, modern as much as opulent. Their subtle colors, contributing shimmer and reflected light, are better suited as striking accents in stencils or as part of a decorative finish than for application over large areas.

The walls of this bedroom in an oceanfront Southampton, New York, home were encrusted with shells collected in the Caribbean by the owner. Manhattan designer Brian Murphy painted the plaster base white, then tinted it with pearlescent hues to give the space the shimmery feel of water reflecting sunlight.

tips

• Use a roller with a ½-nap to apply textured paints, and a chip brush to fill in any areas that were missed by the roller.

• Use inexpensive disposable brushes—most textured paints and mediums are difficult to remove from brushes after use.

• Sand-textured paint is a great way to conceal small cracks and minor imperfections on older walls.

BASE: Pumpkin Cream 2168-20
GLAZE: Peach Cobbler 2169-40

textured paint

Textured paint gives plain walls instant patina and personality reminiscent of an old stone structure, and is especially suitable for an entrance hall, sunroom, or mudroom. The rough finish also incidentally disguises less-than-perfect surfaces. To add color, these paints can be tinted with universal tints (see page 160), latex paint, or, as we did here, simply painted over—a color wash is a perfect way to impart a sun-bleached weathered look.

SAND-TEXTURED COLOR-WASHED WALLS

1 **MASK ALL WALLS** adjacent to where you'll be working with blue or green low-tack painter's tape. Prime the walls if necessary and let dry.

2 **PICK UP A GENEROUS** amount of sand texture paint on a chip brush. Apply one coat of white-pigmented sand-textured paint using random crisscrossing strokes. Allow approximately 5 hours to dry.

3 **APPLY THE BASE COAT** with a roller or chip brush. Maneuver within the crevices of the textured surface to get complete coverage. Let dry.

4 **PREPARE THE GLAZE** by adding 3 parts glaze to 1 part water and 1 part paint (in the glaze color) in a bucket and mixing thoroughly. Mix in glaze extender as needed (see page 62). Pour a small amount of the mixture into a paint tray.

5 **WITH A FRESH CHIP BRUSH**, whisk on the glaze in a random crisscross motion, moving across the wall and overlapping brushstrokes. Work quickly. Use the brush to catch drips from time to time. Let dry overnight.

LEVEL
Beginner
(passionate novice)

NUMBER OF PEOPLE
1 or 2

SPECIALTY TOOLS
• Two $\frac{1}{2}$-inch nap rollers
• Two to three 4-inch chip brushes

PREPARATION
As you would for any painting project, prepare the surface and mask off the ceiling, baseboards, doors, and window trim.

To arrive at the satiny, lustrous finish of Venetian plaster, it's essential to begin with smooth walls. After that, the skill is all in troweling on the plaster as evenly and thinly as possible, without overworking or scratching the finish, and in burnishing to a perfectly smooth result. Venetian plaster is available in different colors and in high gloss or matte finish.

MARBLE-LOOK VENETIAN PLASTER

1 **MASK ALL WALLS** adjacent to where you'll be working with blue or green low-tack painter's tape. Prime the walls; the surface should be clean, dry and, above all, as smooth as possible.

2 **WITH A VENETIAN PLASTER** spatula or trowel, apply a thin coat (about $\frac{1}{16}$th-inch thick) of undercoat foundation as smoothly and evenly as possible, minimizing ridge marks. Let dry for 4 to 6 hours. Sand with 100 grit followed by 320 grit sandpaper (wear a respirator or dust mask) and remove any dust with a damp cloth. The end result should be an extremely smooth surface.

3 **LIFT A SMALL AMOUNT** of Venetian plaster onto the tip and edge of the spatula. Holding it at a 5- to 10-degree angle, spread the Venetian plaster very thinly using short random strokes over 3-foot areas at a time. Don't worry if you don't have complete coverage, the second or third coats will "fill in" empty spaces. Allow to dry for the time specified by the manufacturer's instructions.

4 **FRAGMENTS OF DRIED PLASTER** will very easily scratch this finish, so keep the plaster pail covered with the lid or a damp cloth at all times. Clean the spatula periodically; to remove any residue, dip the tool in water and wipe off with a thick cellulose sponge.

5 **GENTLY RUN THE SPATULA** over the surface to smooth away any ridges. If necessary, lightly sand with 320 or 600 grit sandpaper. Apply a second and, for darker colors, a third layer of plaster with random curved strokes.

6 **AFTER THE FINAL LAYER** of plaster has been applied, polish immediately with the flat side of the spatula or trowel.

7 **APPLY A THIN,** even clear wax topcoat for a high-gloss finish or to give added protection to areas that may be exposed to high traffic or to water. With the spatula, pull firmly across the wall with random strokes. Let dry to the touch.

LEVEL
Expert
(trained and experienced)

NUMBER OF PEOPLE:
1 or 2 for a large space

SPECIALTY TOOLS
- Venetian plaster metal spatulas with rounded corners (package of 4 sizes; see page 000), or stainless steel trowels
- Undercoat foundation (special preformulated Venetian plaster primer coat)
- 100, 320, and 600 grit sandpaper
- Venetian plaster (premixed smooth)
- Thick cellulose sponge
- Protective finishing wax (acrylic-based wax is recommended)

APPLICATION METHOD
See page 156.

PREPARATION
As you would for any painting project, prepare the surface and mask off the ceiling, baseboards, doors, and window trim.

OPPOSITE
Temptation 1609

variations

1 "SCRAFFITO" STRIÉ

The charm of this effect from Alpha Workshops is in its child-like irregularities, but practice beforehand as you have to work very quickly. Tape off 3-foot-wide sections, apply the glaze and use a chip brush to create a rough strié. With an eraser tool (see page 149) or pencil eraser, "draw" vertical and zigzag lines through the glaze, exposing the yellow base coat.

BASE: Yellow Highlighter 202I-40

GLAZE: Burnt Caramel 2167-10

2 AGED PLASTER

Prime the walls and let dry. Mix two parts dry wall compound and two parts texture paint to one part base color. Spread in random crisscross motions with a Venetian plaster spatula or trowel. Let dry and repeat until you've got the look you want. Apply the glaze with a brush; it will puddle in the low areas creating contrast with the lighter, raised surfaces.

COLOR: Soft Chinchilla 2135-50

3 POLKA DOTS

Apply three thin layers of Venetian plaster following the method on page 127. Place a circle stencil on the surface. With a 3-inch trim roller, roll on a thin coat of plaster across the stencil. Apply a second coat with a spatula or trowel. Work from the edges inward to avoid seepage. Remove the stencil and lightly sand the edges of

1 **"SCRAFFITO" STRIÉ**

2 AGED PLASTER

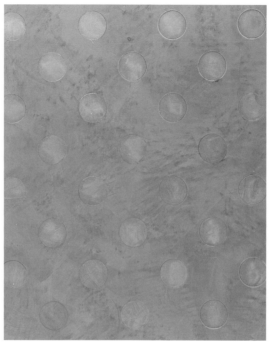

3 POLKA DOTS

4 GRASS CLOTH WEAVE

5 CLOUDY VENETIAN PLASTER

each raised area with 200 grit sandpaper to smooth. Wax and buff with 0000 steel wool.

VENETIAN PLASTER BASE COAT:
Steel Blue 823
VENETIAN PLASTER TOPCOAT:
Blue Nova 825

4 GRASS CLOTH WEAVE

Apply a coat of Venetian plaster (see page 127). Allow to dry. Thin the Venetian plaster slightly with water and apply a second layer with a chip brush. Work the plaster into the bristles on an artist's paper palette. (Mist with water to thin it down as necessary.) Work across the wall in broad horizontal strokes. Let dry. Repeat using the same color, in broad vertical strokes to create a crosshatched effect. Finish with a coat of wax colored slightly darker than the base color with universal tint (see page 160). Allow to dry overnight and buff with 0000 steel wool.

VENETIAN PLASTER BASE COAT:
Orange Appeal 124
VENETIAN PLASTER TOPCOAT:
Pan for Gold 181

5 CLOUDY VENETIAN PLASTER

This creates a subtle blend of two colors. Apply two coats of the first color (see page 127). Allow to dry. Apply the second color and wipe randomly with a damp sponge to reveal the first color. Do this the same day so the finish is not fully set. Apply a clear wax followed by a tinted (gray) wax to enhance the effect.

BASE COAT: Sycamore 1137
TOP COAT: White Dove

1 GLIMMERING MIST
Roll on two coats of the base
color and allow to dry. With a
level and ruler draw overlapping rectangles across the wall
in pencil. Tape off about a third
of the rectangles and, starting
with the darkest color, brush
the first glaze on a flat sponge
and apply within the taped-off
rectangles to create a cloudy
effect. Allow to dry. Tape off
another third of the rectangles
and repeat with the next color;
where colors overlap, a third
color will be created. Continue
with the remaining glazes.
BASE: Arctic Blue 2050-60
GLAZES: Silver 20, Icy Mist
PT-280, Brushed Radiance
PT-300

2 JEWELED STRIÉ
Metallic glazes produce very
beautiful strié finishes. Roll on
two coats of the base color.
Following directions for a regular strie (see page 75), roll on
the silver glaze; starting at the
top of the wall, drag down with
a chip brush to create this
jeweled effect.
BASE: Blue Calypso 727
GLAZE: Silver 20

3 SHIMMERING STRIPES
Random overlapping colors
create these layerered stripes.
Roll on two coats of the base
color; this will be the widest
stripe. Apply the widest tape to
the wall, then tear one edge;
continue across the wall, spacing informally. Roll on glaze 1,
then remove the tape. Let dry.
For the second stripe, overlap

1 GLIMMERING MIST

2 JEWELED STRIÉ

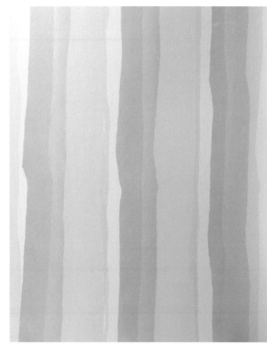

3 SHIMMERING STRIPES

4 MOSAIC BORDER

5 PEARLESCENT RECTANGLES

the first stripe with tape and tear again. Roll on the second glaze. Use your accent color in the narrowest strip.

BASE: Marble White OC-34
GLAZE 1: Silver 20
GLAZE 2: Pearlescent White 01
ACCENT: Compassion PT-110

4 MOSAIC BORDER

Keep most of your colors within the same tone, using a few accent colors. Tape off the outside border of the mosaic. Use a small chip brush to randomly paint in several blocks of color. With an artist's brush, paint the border and grout lines across and around these color blocks to create the appearance of broken tile. The metallic silver and peach colors were added as accents to give the effect some dimension.

BASE: White Dove OC-17
TILES: Maritime White OC-5, Fog Mist OC-31, Harbor Haze 2136-60, Silver 20
GROUT: Graystone 1475
BORDER AND ACCENTS: Harbor Haze 2136-60

5 PEARLESCENT RECTANGLES

Roll on two coats of the base color. Rag on the glaze. Let dry. Randomly tape off a design of rectangles in a pleasing pattern and paint. Let dry then tape off any overlapping rectangles and paint.

BASE: Pale Petal 1178
GLAZE: Sailor's Delight 1296
RECTANGLES: Pearlescent White 01, Compassion PT-110, Endearing Pink PT-170

on location: french connection

EVERY DETAIL OF THIS FRENCH-STYLE FARMHOUSE in upstate New York, from the herb-and-flower-filled parterre to mellowed plaster walls and limestone fireplace, rings with Gallic authenticity. Yet much of that detail was created by owner and designer Carolyn Guttilla, an accomplished decorative painter.

The house is laid out almost entirely on one level, with a ninety-foot, sun-drenched great room at its heart. A rounded tower at one end houses two second-floor guest rooms. Graceful French doors open along the length of the first floor to a large patio and carefully composed gardens. Guttilla hand-painted all the custom-built cabinetry in the house, from closets to baths to kitchen, with a variety of techniques. The cupboards in the master bath, for example, are painted to match the honeyed tones of the travertine tile on the floor and shower. And in every room, the colors have a soft, time-worn quality that echo the old stone and aged plaster and wood of their European inspiration.

But the central great room may be the best example of Guttilla's use of decorative technique to age and mellow the new house. The soaring tongue-and-groove ceiling is stained a soft sage green, while the walls are creased and lined with an elaborate effect that looks precisely like old plaster. "There was so much wall space that it would have been deadly to make it all white," says the designer, "so I developed my own technique to give it some patina." The procedure involved painting a white base coat, then layering shades of taupe onto a large swath of canvas and smoothing it onto the wall like a kind of frottage. After peeling it off, Guttilla ran a roller loaded with more white paint over the still-wet patches, feathering and blending the colors into a mottled, tactile surface, with the restful tones of antique whitewash.

The fireplace that dominates one end of the room is also something of an optical illusion. To create the look, Guttilla razored old paintbrushes almost down to the ferrule, leaving only a half inch of irregular stubble. She mixed a palette of pale grays, taupes, russets, and white, dipped a brush in several colors

at a time, and with an index finger stroked the edge of the bristles to release a fine spray of paint. The result is a pale faux limestone so realistic that it's almost impossible to tell it apart from the actual limestone firebox it surrounds.

"It's easier to see a home's structure and architecture when it's not competing with outrageous color and brilliant walls," says Guttilla. "And I love the French look that is both very serene and extremely studied. I think that's what this house communicates."

THIS PAGE
The plasterlike walls of the great room were created with the designer's own technique of laying on paint with a piece of wrinkled canvas, then feathering in additional colors with a roller to create the mottled veins of old plaster.
BASE: Super White 02
GLAZE: Sandlot Gray 2107-50

OPPOSITE
The light, airy colors of the mantel, with its display of creamware, make a lovely counterpoint to the massive shapes and weight of the hearth. The faux limestone, created by slowly spattering every inch of the mantel by hand, is almost indistinguishable from the real thing on the rest of the hearth.
BASE:
Big Bend Beige AC-37
GLAZES:
Grand Teton White AC-42,
Cream Yellow 2155-60,
Elephant Tusk OC-8,
Ebony King 2132-20,
Gettysburg Gray HC-107

NEWPORT REMEMBERED Abrams

THE PRIVATE WORLD OF THE DUKE AND DUCHESS OF WINDSOR
HUGO VICKERS

OSCAR DE LA RENTA ASSOULINE

faux finishes 7

Faux finishes are almost a discipline unto themselves; unlike other finishes they are intended to deceive, imitating everything from bird's eye maple to carrara marble. While they can be demanding and time-consuming, at their simplest they involve layering two or more glazing techniques introduced earlier in this book—basic wood graining can be done by a combination of strié and flogging, for example. Since the goal is verisimilitude, it's essential to have a sample of the material you're copying on hand. And bear in mind that these finishes look best when used where the real thing might be found: A faux marble mantel is more believable than a faux marble door.

The clean lines and subtle palette enlivened with touches of color in the entry hall of Suzanne Kasler's home sets the tone for the rest of the house. A faux limestone finish by Scarlet Jimison gives the space a cool and airy feel, particularly welcome in the hot Southern climate.

wood graining

LEVEL
Expert
(trained and experienced)

NUMBER OF PEOPLE
1

SPECIALTY TOOLS
• Flogger
• Small artist's brush
• Several chip brushes in
  various sizes
• House-painting brush
• Hake brush

APPLICATION METHOD
See page 156.

PREPARATION
Prepare the walls. Mask off
the ceiling, baseboards, doors,
and window trim. Apply a
primer coat and let dry.
  Apply two coats of eggshell
base coat paint. Allow approximately 12 hours to dry.

OPPOSITE TOP:
BASE: Autumn Orange 2156-10
GLAZES: Autumn Bronze
2162-10,
Grizzly Brown 2111-20,
Taupe 2110-10

OPPOSITE BOTTOM:
BASE: Hathaway Gold 194
GLAZE: Country Lane 2088-20

At its finest, faux wood graining is a challenging technique that can take years to master, but understanding basic principles can help you achieve some believable results. The step-by-step instructions below, for a small walnut cabinet door, give you a general introductory approach to wood graining; you can easily apply these same steps to a larger door or even paneling.

WOOD-GRAIN CABINET DOOR

1 MASK ALL SURFACES adjacent to where you'll be working with blue or green low-tack painter's tape. Prime the surface, then apply the base coat color with a roller.

2 PREPARE THE FIRST glaze color by thoroughly mixing 4 parts glaze and 1 part paint. (Because this is a small area, no glaze extender is needed.)

3 PREPARE THE SECOND glaze color by thoroughly mixing 4 parts glaze and 1 part paint. (Because this is a small area, no glaze extender is needed.) Put aside.

4 BEGIN WORK ON the center panel. Tape all adjacent areas with blue or green low-tack tape.

5 APPLY THE FIRST GLAZE vertically with a house-painting brush, brushing several times to smooth out the strokes.

6 WHILE THE GLAZE is still wet, create the pores of the wood: Hold the handle of the flogger approximately $\frac{1}{2}$ inch from the ferrule with the bristles upright. Working from bottom to top, slap the wet glaze with the heel of the bristles (see page 156). Complete the area and let dry.

7 APPLY THE SECOND glaze with a chip brush and pull vertically through the glaze to create a strié grain effect. Allow to dry.

8 BEGIN WORK ON the stiles (vertical borders). Tape all adjacent areas with blue or green low-tack painter's tape. Repeat steps 5 and 6. Allow to dry.

9 APPLY THE SECOND glaze to the stiles with a chip brush, pulling through vertically to create a strié grain effect. Allow to dry.

FAUX WALNUT Layering colors and techniques is essential to achieving a sense of depth and realism.

FANTASY GRAINING A diamond-pattern, heart-grain inlay in whimsical colors produced using a graining heel.

10 **BEGIN WORK ON** the rails (horizontal borders). Tape all adjacent areas with blue or green low-tack painter's tape. Repeat step 5 using horizontal strokes. Repeat step 6, flogging from right to left, always moving toward the bristles. Let dry.

11 **APPLY THE SECOND GLAZE** to the rails with a chip brush, pulling through horizontally to create a strié grain effect.

12 **DARKEN THE SECOND GLAZE** with acrylic paint (see page 160). Starting in the center of the panel, paint the irregular "mountain" shapes associated with the heart grain (center) of the wood using a small artist's brush. Alternatively, use a "heel" to create the heart grain (see page 156). Very lightly soften the shapes with a hake brush (see page 152). Add vertical straight graining on either side, making a gradual transition. (The farther from the heart, the straighter the strié lines.)

13 **TO ADD DEPTH** or to adjust the color, mix a third glaze color. Apply a thin layer over the entire surface, brushing several times to smooth out the strokes.

14 **SEAL ALL PAINTED** surfaces with a water-based satin, semi-gloss, or high-gloss topcoat to even out the surface and provide a sheen.

tips

- Not all woods have heart grain. You can produce a credible wood finish just by combining strié and flogging.

- Almost any coarse, long-bristled brush can be used for strié or flogging to create wood-grain effects. A shorter-bristled wallpaper brush, inexpensive 4-inch chip brush, or standard house-painting brush can also be used effectively. Practice with them on a sample board to choose the right one for each project.

| # limestone blocks

LEVEL
Intermediate
(patient and talented)

NUMBER OF PEOPLE
1

SPECIALTY TOOLS
- Plenty of newspaper
- Rolls of ¼-inch tape
- Single-edge razor blades to score the tape
- X-acto knife or box cutter
- Foam rollers and foam brushes

PREPARATION
As you would for any painting project, prepare the surface and mask off the ceiling, baseboards, doors, and window trim.

Faux stone effects are created by layering techniques, from mottling on (page 65) and spattering (page 155) to ragging (page 69). The technique used here is frottage (sometimes known as smooshing), in which a wet glaze is applied to a surface and blotted with a material such as newpaper or plastic, leaving a distinctive texture (see page 152). Working in individual blocks bordered by grout lines makes for an easily managed area that you can stop and start without having to worry about keeping a wet edge.

LIMESTONE BLOCKS

1 MASK ALL WALLS adjacent to where you'll be working with blue or green low-tack painter's tape. Prime the walls if necessary, apply two coats of satin base color, and let dry for approximately 8 hours or overnight. This will be the grout color.

2 ON GRAPH PAPER, draw the walls to scale and layout the stone block pattern (see page 106). Using your drawing as a guide, transfer this layout to the walls with a chalk snap line or pencil and level.

3 USING 1/4-INCH GRAPHIC TAPE, tape the grout lines of the blocks on the wall. Grout lines can range in thickness from a simple pencil line to one inch or even wider; ¼ inch is a typical width.

4 PREPARE THE GLAZE coat by thoroughly mixing 4 parts glaze and 1 part paint in a bucket. Pour a small amount of the mixture into a paint tray.

5 APPLY THE GLAZE with a foam brush or roller one block at a time. Lightly press a crumpled sheet of newspaper, just large enough to cover the area you're working on, onto the glaze. Move your fingers over the paper, "tickling" the surface to manipulate the glaze, this is known as frottage. Peel off the newspaper. This will leave a texture similar to real stone. Repeat until you get the degree of texture you want.

6 CONTINUE AROUND the room in this manner. Let dry. Remove the tape to reveal the grout lines.

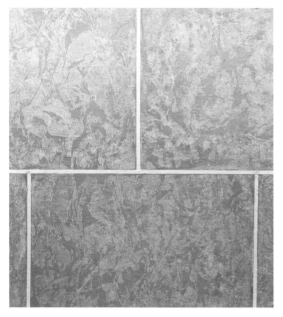

LIMESTONE BLOCKS The technique known as "frottage" may be the simplest and quickest way to achieve a faux stone effect. Variations within each block only add to the realism of the effect. Use several colors to build up the depth of the finish.

TEXTURED LIMESTONE 1 Apply the base color and tape the grout lines. Roll on tinted textured paint (several coats may be necessary to build the finish). Use three different colors for the blocks. Remove the tape to reveal the grout.

tips

- As long as the glaze remains wet, you can reapply the newspaper and manipulate it to give the stone effect more complexity.

- Try other materials for removing the glaze, such as tissue paper, plastic wrap, or a brown paper bag.

- Using a second glaze color in a slightly lighter or darker value will add greater depth and interest to the effect.

TEXTURED LIMESTONE 2 Apply the base color before taping. Trowel on a mix of three quarters dry wall compound with one quarter plaster of Paris then press crumpled cooking foil and pieces of shells into the finish. Apply a glaze of the base color and partially remove with cheesecloth.

GRANITE Apply two coats of the base color then tape out the grout lines. Sponge the blocks in three colors, allow to dry. Spatter on a darker fourth color before removing the tape.

marbling

LEVEL
Expert
(trained and experienced)

RECOMMENDED ON
Any clean, smooth, small area

NUMBER OF PEOPLE
1

SPECIALTY TOOLS
- Sea sponge
- Small long-haired veining brush, turkey feather, and/or script liner
- Hake brush
- Four 1-pint deli containers with lids
- Two 1-quart deli containers with lids
- Paper artist's palette
- Egg carton

PREPARATION
As you would for any painting project, prepare the surface and mask off the ceiling, baseboards, doors, and window trim.

Simulating marble requires expertise in using a combination of basic glazing techniques, including mottling, stippling, ragging, and spattering, as well as a familiarity with veining tools (see page 157). As with other faux techniques, it's essential to have a sample on hand to refer to as you create the finish. Generally, faux marble looks more realistic on small areas such as fireplace mantels, baseboards (as described here), and chair rails rather than large expanses of wall.

WHITE CARRARA BASEBOARD

1 **MASK OFF THE** baseboard with blue or green low-tack painter's tape. Prime if necessary, apply two coats of semi-gloss base color, and let dry for approximately 8 hours or overnight. To create grout lines, place ⅛-inch tape vertically every 3 feet around the baseboard.

2 **PREPARE THE WHITE** glaze by mixing 4 parts glaze and 1 part paint in a quart container. Mix in glaze extender as needed (see page 62). This will be the main color of the marble.

3 **PREPARE THE REMAINING** four glazes, each in a 1-pint container, by thoroughly mixing 4 parts glaze and 1 part paint. Transfer a teaspoonful of each onto an artist's paper palette.

4 **WITH A CHIP BRUSH,** apply a generous layer of the white glaze to a 3-foot section of the baseboard. Using a damp sea sponge, move the glaze into soft drifts across the surface in one direction until you have eliminated all brush strokes.

5 **WHILE THE SURFACE** is still wet, blend two or three of the glazes on the palette with a small veining brush, turkey feather, or script liner, then apply to the drifts. Use a hake brush to soften any hard applications of color (see page 152) and blend the undertones; wipe the bristles frequently with a rag to keep them from becoming stiff. Repeat using a different combination of glazes (all will be variations of gray) until you have a realistic-looking marble base. Allow to dry.

6 **APPLY A THIN LAYER** of the white glaze over the entire surface. With a piece of cheesecloth, pounce all over to remove glaze in order to allow some veining to show through more than others.

7 **FOR ADDED DEPTH,** use watered-down base coat white paint, then apply with a veining brush to create "fissures" that cross the existing veins.

8 **APPLY TWO COATS** of water-based polyurethane for sheen and protection.

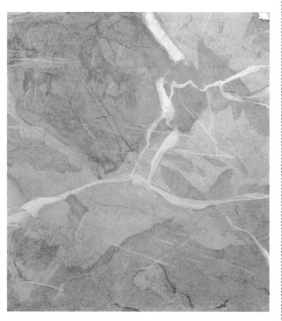

1 CARRARA MARBLE One of the most popular marbles, the pale colors of Carrara are more forgiving making this also one of the easiest marbles to execute well. Blending and softening are key techniques to achieving a good result.

2 ROJO ALICANTE This style of marble exhibits a higher contrast in the background glazes. Larger veins are added with a script liner; a feather is used for more random veining.

3 NOTRE DAME Apply the glaze and stipple off with cheesecloth to even out the texture. Spatter with alcohol and wisk lightly with a hake brush to reveal the base color. Apply feint veins with a brush. Finally, lightly spatter on a darker glaze.

4 PYRENESE PORTER Apply a black glaze over a gray base; pull the glaze off with cheesecloth and soften the effect with a hake brush. Use several colors in the veining and apply a high gloss finish to add a realism to the result.

tips

- Always use a piece of real marble as a guide.

- The more "movement" in the undertones of texture and color, the more depth you create and the more realistic the effect.

- When deciding on the base coat color, look for the lightest color in the real marble (other than the white veins).

- Use a turkey feather instead of a brush to create a less controlled, more naturalistic look to the veins.

1 CARRARA MARBLE
BASE: Dove Wing OC-18
VEINING: Nimbus Grey 2131-50

2 ROJO ALICANTE
BASE: Pirates Cove Peach 903
GLAZE: Sedona Clay 2174-30, Dusty Mauve 2174-40, Peach Blossom 2175-50

3 NOTRE DAME
BASE: Beacon Hill Damask HC-2
GLAZE: Rich Clay Brown 2164-30, Earth Russet 2173-10

4 PYRENESE PORTER
BASE: Purple Lotus 2072-30
GLAZE: Galaxy 2117-20
VEINING: Venetian Gold 2158-20, Pale Celery 2150-60

on location: going with the grain

THIS ELEGANT LITTLE JEWEL BOX of an apartment began life as three formal parlors in an 1850s New York townhouse. By the time architect Gil Schafer acquired it, the years and a succession of tenants had taken their toll in the form of modernist additions and clumsy renovations. But with his disciplined sensibility, trained eye, and love of neoclassical detail, Schafer was able to reclaim the altered space and imbue it with a sense of its original dignity.

The process began with the imposition of architectural balance. The space is small—only 900 square feet—but the ceilings are an impressive 13 feet high, so Schafer added two weighty, classic columns at one end to accentuate the soaring ceiling and opposing 12-foot windows. Next came recessed moldings, custom-detailed door frames, plaster ceiling medallions, and a black scagliola mantelpiece, with fluted columns and a Greek key frieze, to replace a stock marble hearth.

The massive double doors that open into the main living-dining area are perhaps the best example of artisanal skill. Almost 10 feet tall, the paneled doors are entirely done in a faux mahogany finish, with exquisite handpainted wood graining and ebonized borders.

"I wanted mahogany doors, but to buy beautiful crotch-grained doors would have been too costly," says Schafer. "The idea of faux grain fit with the historical basis of the interior—people often used that technique when a certain wood wasn't accessible or was too expensive."

The doors took more than two weeks to complete, in an elaborate multistep process that involved multiple coats of paint, glaze, and varnish, with detail added incrementally in watercolor and artist's acrylics. The decorative painter, Jean Carrau, is a fifth-generation artisan, who learned the technique by working alongside his father and studying and teaching in France and Belgium.

The surrounding walls were also given their share of attention: the surfaces were done by Weidl Associates in a rich terra-cotta cross-hatched glaze, which echoes the luxurious, auburn tones of the doors. The subtle, gridlike effect is in keeping with the rigorous sensibility of the space, and the deep color is the perfect backdrop for Schafer's extensive art collection.

"From the doors to the wall glazing, this whole apartment is very much about working with different artists and their skills," says Schafer. "Respect for craft is what made it all come together."

THIS PAGE:
The deep, lustrous tones of the faux-grain mahogany doors are a tribute to the skill of French decorative painter Jean Carrau. To complete the look, the panel borders were ebonized, and all of the hardware was custom-made in patinated brass with cobalt glass knobs.

OPPOSITE:
A rich apricot glaze echoes the complex, earthy shades of the doors and wood tones of the antique table. The finish is a cross-hatched strié which adds depth and texture within a crisp framework.
BASE: Soft Beige 2156-60
GLAZE: Jack O'lantern 2156-30

tools and paint

tools of the trade

BRUSHES

Most of the techniques in this book don't require a huge investment in exotic equipment, but high-quality brushes really can make a difference and are worth their price (anywhere from $20 upwards). A good brush is balanced, with the weight in the ferrule, or base of the bristles, so it feels comfortable in the hand. It holds more paint, so you don't have to break off midway through a long brush stroke to reload, and won't shed bristles or leave unwanted tracks in the paint. With proper cleaning and care, it can be used again and again.

Latex paint requires a synthetic bristle brush. Natural-bristle brushes shouldn't be used, since the bristles absorb water and the brush will lose its shape and rigidity.

The best synthetic brushes are a combination of nylon filaments, for softness, and polyester filaments, for firmness. These custom-blended brushes hold up well, are easy to clean, and provide exceptional capacity for fast, complete coverage with all types of paints, including oil-based paints. Choose brushes with extra-firm nylon bristles to hold a precise tip when cutting in and with "flagged" bristles to imitate natural hair bristles.

Brushes with all-nylon bristles are durable and easy to clean, but they sometimes soften with prolonged use or in hot temperatures. The soft, precisely processed tips are good for varnishing.

For oil-based paints, glazes, and varnishes, choose a natural white or black (China) bristle brush. The naturally soft, flagged tips help eliminate visible brush marks and create an even, uniform coat.

ROLLERS

Just as with brushes, a high-quality roller will make a difference in your work. Look for a roller with a steel frame and comfortable handle that is threaded to accommodate an extension pole—you'll need one to reach ceilings and other high places. Make sure the cage of the roller is flexible but strong, so that it is easy to put on and get off, but won't work loose when you are painting.

For latex paints, choose a shed-resistant, knit polyester roller cover or one made with lamb's wool. For alkyd and oil-based paints, use a lamb's wool, mohair, or synthetic roller cover. Polyester/lamb's wool rollers have a high paint capacity, leave an exceptionally smooth finish, and are recommended for flat or satin finish paints. They are an affordable alternative to 100% lamb's wool rollers, which have the highest paint capacity and smoothest finish of all rollers and can be used with all paints and stains.

Shed-resistant rollers have individual fibers woven through the backing to ensure lint-free finishes. They work best on smooth to semi-smooth finishes.

Always choose a roller without obvious seams or loose fibers; seams leave streaks and loose fibers come off in the paint. Choose a nap size (fiber length) appropriate to your project; a general rule of thumb is the smoother the surface being painted, the shorter the nap. So for sheetrock, smooth plaster, wood, and metal, you would use a short nap of $\frac{1}{4}$ inch to $\frac{3}{8}$ inch; for medium surfaces, such as lightly textured wood and masonry, $\frac{3}{8}$ inch to $\frac{1}{2}$ inch; for rough surfaces, such as brick, concrete or stucco, $\frac{3}{4}$ inch to 1 inch.

PRECEDING PAGE
Inspired by its location on a saltwater pond, decorator Lynn Morgan used a palette of watery blues and greens throughout this 19th century Colonial in Connecticut. Shelly Denning painted the checkerboard pattern on the entrance hall floor in a gray-blue.
COLOR: Heaven On Earth 1661

Foam rollers don't hold a lot of paint, glaze, or varnish, and they have a tendency to create tiny bubbles on the surface, resulting in unsightly air pockets. But used carefully their size makes them well suited to painting small areas, such as cabinet doors or stripes in a geometric finish.

DECORATIVE PAINTING BRUSHES (photograph page 148)

Brushes are to the decorative painter what knives are to a chef: the single most important tools of the profession, chosen with care and jealously guarded. Just as a chef has a collection of culinary knives, each for a specific task, a decorative painter has a wide assortment of brush types, sizes, and shapes. Some are extremely expensive and deliver precise, professional results. Others, more modest in price, work just fine for simpler techniques. But even old and damaged brushes are still useful to create irregular lines in faux techniques and stippled finishes.

ANGLED BRUSH (1) Angled painter's brushes, or trim brushes, are used to cut a base coat or glaze into corners.

ARTIST'S BRUSHES (8 & 9) Indispensable for freehand detail work, touch-ups, veining, lining, and freehand painting. They come in shapes ranging from fine and flat to round and angled, and in sizes #000, #00, #0, and #2.

BADGER BLENDER (5 & 18) A natur hair brush designed to soften and blend colors. It's used primarily for faux marble and wood finishes. A less expensive substitute is the hake brush.

CHIP BRUSH (19) Disposable, inexpensive, and versatile, they're available in 1-, 2-, 3-, and 4-inch sizes. The bristles are usually made of very stiff polyester, so they aren't good at blending, but they work for strié and stippling into corners and tight spots. The 1-inch size is good for mixing up small amounts of glaze and doing sample boards and color tests.

DAGGER BRUSH (11) Similar to a script liner. Used for veining and detail work.

FAN BRUSH (16) Named for its distinctive fan shape, this small brush is used to smooth out small areas of glaze or for veining in faux marble. It can also be used to produce fine wood grain effects.

FITCH BRUSH (12) A hog's hair brush used mainly for marbleizing, freehand, and spatter work in oils. It comes in many shapes; the round ones are excellent for stippling into corners.

FLOGGER (14) A long-bristled horsehair brush used to create the small textured effects that replicate the pores in wood graining. It's fairly costly; you can achieve similar effects with any long-haired strié brush.

FOAM BRUSH (3) Disposable and inexpensive, foam brushes are perfect for dabbing glaze into corners and other small touchups.

GLAZING BRUSH (15) Any large, soft-bristled brush. Used to apply glaze or for dry brushing.

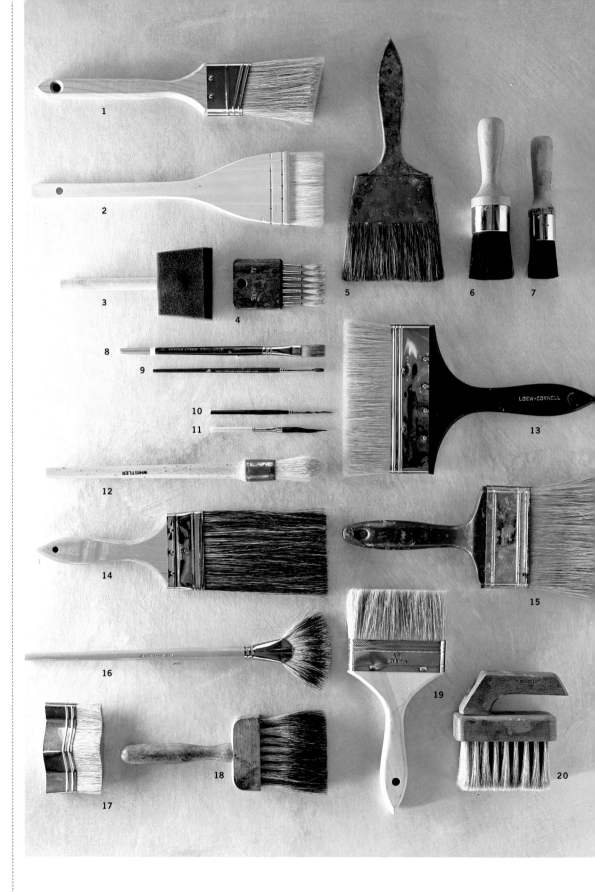

BRUSHES USED IN DECORATIVE PAINTING

1 Angled Brush
2 Hake Brush
3 Foam Brush
4 Pencil Grainer
5 & 18 Badger Blender
6 & 7 Stencil Brushes
8 & 9 Artist's Brushes
10 Script Liner
11 Dagger Brush
12 Fitch Brush
13 Hard-bristle Brush
14 Flogger
15 Glazing Brush
16 Fan Brush
17 Wavy Mottler
19 Chip Brush
20 Stipple Brush

HAKE BRUSH (2) A unique flat, wide brush, ideal for applying glaze media over large areas. It's especially suited for marbling or wood-graining techniques. The flat hand and the select soft sheep hair allow for excellent brush control.

HARD-BRISTLE BRUSH (13) Especially useful for strié to create continuous lines through the glaze.

PENCIL GRAINER (4) With several bristle heads set in one handle, this brush is used to create the wood grain effects found in bird's eye maple and mahogany.

SCRIPT LINER (10) A small, long-haired round brush used for veining, particularly in oak, detail work, and painting long, thin strokes.

STENCIL BRUSHES (6 & 7) Blunt, cylindrical, short-handled stencil brushes are designed to cleanly apply a small amount of paint into the negative space of a stencil.

STIPPLE BRUSH (20) Often made with stiff hog or horsehair bristles set in a wide horizontal handle. It comes in many different sizes; use small ones to reach into awkward areas and larger sizes for walls and ceilings.

WAVY MOTTLER (17) Mostly used in wood graining to create another layer of texture.

SPECIALTY PAINTING TOOLS
(Photograph page 151)

ARTIST'S PAPER PALETTE (18) Used for paint and glaze color tests and to offload excess paint from a stencil brush, rubber or foam stamp, or foam roller. Tear off and dispose the top sheet when it becomes messy or full.

CHECK ROLLER (19) Typically used in wood-graining or glaze finishes to produce a textured effect.

CHEESECLOTH (20) Standard cheese-cloth, available in most hardware or commercial paint stores, is an essential tool for applying or removing glaze coats. Can be used as a substi-tute for a rag in almost any decorative finish.

ERASER TOOL (7&8) Use the rubber angled tips to "wipe out" marks in a glaze, and reveal color underneath. Applications include erasing vein lines in marbleizing or creating free-hand designs through a thin veil of glaze. The tips come in many shapes and sizes, from a small, brushlike point up to a 1-inch-wide "spatula." An ordinary pink eraser cut into the shape you want makes an adequate substitute.

FOAM HOTDOG ROLLER (5) A narrow roller for stenciling or whenever you want paint or glaze to have a smoother finish than can be obtained with a standard roller with a ¼-inch nap. It's also slightly easier to clean.

GRAINING HEEL (13 & 14) A grooved rubber tool that is dragged through glaze with a

tip

HOUSEHOLD TOOLS
• Some decorative techniques require the use of specialized tools, but ordinary household items can be used to create interesting effects. Motifs for stamping can be cut from kitchen sponges or upholstery foam. A coarse strié can be created with steel wool. For a bold graining pattern, try an inexpensive hand or whisk broom.

rocking motion of the wrist to make the natural-looking heart grain and knot patterns characteristic of wood graining. Also called a rocker.

METAL COMBS (23-25) Metal combs produce "hard" precise lines, for a more manufactured look than rubber combing. Primarily used for wood graining; sometimes used for strié and to mimic fabric weaves such as linen and denim.

MYLAR FILM (12) A thin polyester film used to make stencils. The designs are drawn or traced onto the frosted side of the film and cut out with an X-acto knife.

RUBBER COMB (15) A triangular comb featuring different tooth sizes. It is commonly used in wood graining techniques, producing smooth, natural-looking grain lines.

RUBBER SQUEEGEE COMB (22) Buy precut or cut a standard window squeegee with a pair of pinking shears to create jagged "teeth." This is a handy tool for creating combing patterns.

RUBBER STAMP (1 & 2) Motifs are laser-cut from rubber and permanently mounted on wood blocks for comfortable handling when stamping over large areas. A thin coat of paint on the stamp ensures a sharp image.

SEA SPONGE (21) Natural sea sponges are used in positive and negative mottling, or sponging, techniques. Irregular shapes and large pores create a more open effect; smaller holes make for a tighter, less airy look.

SPATTER STICK (17) A plain wooden mixing stick; some specialized versions are available at art supply stores. Used in spatter techniques by lightly tapping a paint-loaded brush against it.

STEEL WOOL (3) Coarse steel wool creates a more rustic, casual strié than a brush.

TOOTHBRUSH (6) Draw a fingertip across it and an ordinary toothbrush becomes a specialty spattering tool, delivering a fine spray. Dip the bristles into paint or glaze for additive techniques, water (with latex glazes) or solvent (with oil-based glazes) for subtractive techniques.

TRIM ROLLER (4) In combination with a trim (angled) brush, a trim roller is used for painting or applying base coat around the perimeter of walls, ceilings, and any areas where a standard 7- or 9-inch roller cannot reach. It can also be used in striping when the stripes are narrower than a standard roller width.

TURKEY FEATHER (16) Long and pliable, often used in country graining for removing glaze in fanlike patterns. It's also used in marbleizing techniques for applying veins and drifts of color.

VENETIAN PLASTER SPATULA (10 & 11) Flexible metal spatula used to apply and spread thin layers Venetian plaster.

X-ACTO KNIFE (9) Essential for cutting stencils and tape. Run the knife blade against a straight edge when you need to cut a straight line. Keep extra blades on hand and replace the blade when it starts getting dull.

Venetian Plaster Trowel

SPECIALTY PAINTING TOOLS

1 & 2 Rubber Stamp
3 Steel Wool
4 Trim Roller
5 Foam Hotdog Roller
6 Toothbrush
7 & 8 Eraser Tool
9 X-acto Knife
10 & 11 Venetian Plaster Spatula
12 Mylar Film
13 & 14 Graining Heel
15 Rubber Comb
16 Turkey Feather
17 Spatter Stick
18 Artist's Paper Palette
19 Check Roller
20 Cheesecloth
21 Sea Sponge
22 Rubber Squeegee Comb
23-25 Metal Combs

COLOR WASHING
BASE: Orange Blossom 2168-30
GLAZE: White

DRY BRUSHING
BASE: Acorn Yellow 2161-40
GLAZE: White

COLOR WASHING

Using a 3- to 4-inch-wide house-painting brush, whisk a generous amount of glaze on to the surface in random crisscross strokes, overlapping as you go. Pick up any drips with your brush and incorporate them into the next stroke.

DRY BRUSHING

Dip a 3- or 4 inch-wide house-painting brush or chip brush into the paint, then offload it onto an artist's paper palette or newspaper to keep it fairly dry. Apply the paint in crisscross strokes.

FROTTAGE WITH A NEWSPAPER
BASE: White
GLAZE: Mineral Alloy 1622

SOFTENING WITH A HAKE BRUSH
BASE: Rio Rancho Clay 111
GLAZE: White

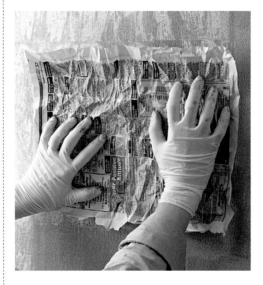

FROTTAGE WITH NEWSPAPER

Press crumpled newpaper lightly onto the glazed surface. Move your fingers from the center out, tickling the surface. Use a fresh sheet each time you move on to another section.

SOFTENING WITH A HAKE BRUSH

With the bristles barely touching the surface, gently whisk this soft-haired brush across the glaze, blending edges of the color as you go.

STRIÉ WITH A HARD-BRISTLE BRUSH

Grip the brush handle and brace your thumb (or index finger if that is more comfortable) against the ferrule to steady it. Press in toward the wall and make long strokes through the wet glaze.

STRIÉ WITH STEEL WOOL

Holding the steel-wool pad between your thumb and four fingers, pull the pad through the glaze, leaving a pattern of coarse lines. Offload excess paint by dabbing, not wiping, the pad on an artist's paper palette.

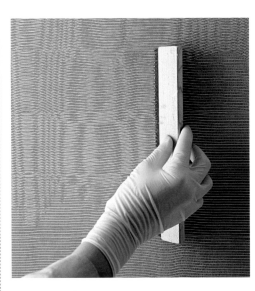

COMBING WITH A RUBBER SQUEEGEE

Hold the comb at an acute angle to the wall and drag through the wet glaze. Wipe off frequently with a damp rag.

COMBING WITH A RUBBER COMB

Hold the comb at an acute angle to the wall and drag through the wet glaze. Wipe off frequently with a damp rag.

STRIÉ WITH A HARD-BRISTLE BRUSH
BASE: White
GLAZE: Cool Blue 2058-40

STRIÉ WITH STEEL WOOL
BASE: White
GLAZE: Brazilian Blue 817

COMBING WITH A RUBBER SQUEEGEE
BASE: White
GLAZE: Rosemary Green 2029-30

COMBING WITH A RUBBER COMB
BASE: White
GLAZE: Citron 2024-30

**MOTTLING ON WITH A
SEA SPONGE**
BASE: Marblehead Gold
HC-11
GLAZE: White

**MOTTLING OFF WITH A
SEA SPONGE**
BASE: Princeton Gold HC-14
GLAZE: White

MOTTLING ON WITH A SEA SPONGE

Dip a damp sponge lightly in the glaze, then offload excess glaze onto an artist's paper palette or newspaper. Holding the sponge lightly as you would a cotton ball, pounce the glaze onto the wall; keep turning the sponge to avoid repetitive marks.

MOTTLING OFF WITH A SEA SPONGE

After the glaze has been applied to the wall, hold and maneuver the sponge in the same fashion as Mottling On. Turn the sponge frequently to avoid repetitive marks. Periodically rinse in water and squeeze dry.

RAG ROLLING
BASE: Soft Pumpkin 2166-40
GLAZE: White
RAGGING OFF
BASE: Richmond Gold HC-41
GLAZE: White

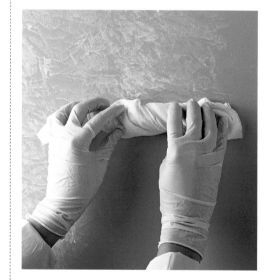

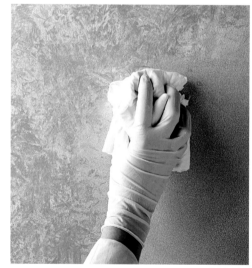

RAG ROLLING

Fold and roll a clean, damp rag into a sausage shape, then slightly twist the center. With both hands, gently roll the rag down or across the wall, lifting glaze as you go. Vary the tightness of the roll to achieve different looks. Change to a clean rag as needed.

RAGGING OFF

Bunch a damp rag in your hand. Holding it lightly, pounce the surface just enough to lift off the wet glaze. Rearrange the rag frequently to prevent repetitive marks. Rinse often or keep a supply of clean rags handy.

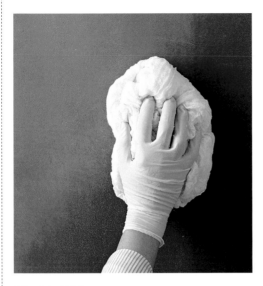

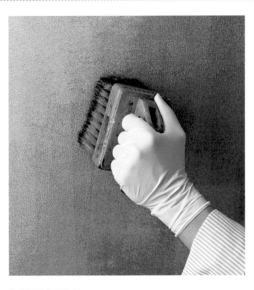

STIPPLING WITH CHEESECLOTH

Bunch the cheesecloth, creating a soft pillow-like shape with one smooth face. Pounce the smooth side on the wall; when it gets saturated with glaze, rearrange it in your hand. Exchange it for a fresh cloth when it's completely saturated.

STIPPLING WITH A STIPPLE BRUSH

Grasp the stipple brush firmly by the handle. Keeping the bristles perpendicular to the wall, pounce the wall surface, leaving a pattern of tiny dots. Wipe the brush regularly with a damp rag.

SPATTERING WITH A TOOTHBRUSH

Stand about 5 inches from the surface and flick back the bristles of a toothbrush loaded with paint with either your thumb or index finger to create a fine spray.

SPATTERING WITH A SPATTER STICK

Hold a brush loaded with paint with its bristles slightly angled toward the wall. Tap the ferrule against the spatter stick, releasing a random spray of paint flecks.

STIPPLING WITH CHEESECLOTH
BASE: White
GLAZE: Ming Jade 2043-20

STIPPLING WITH A STIPPLE BRUSH
BASE: White
GLAZE: Avon Green HC-126

SPATTERING WITH A TOOTHBRUSH
BASE: Heather Gray 2139-40
GLAZE: White

SPATTERING WITH A SPATTER STICK
BASE: Wet Concrete 2114-40
GLAZE: White

**HEART GRAINING
WITH A HEEL**
BASE: Chestertown Buff
HC-9
GLAZE: Dark Mustard
2161-30

FLOGGING
BASE: Rust 2175-30
GLAZE: Grizzly Bear Brown
2111-20

HEART GRAINING WITH A HEEL
Place the top edge of the rubber pattern against the wall. Pull the tool down through the wet glaze while simultaneously rocking it back and forth slowly.

FLOGGING
Grasp the brush approximately an inch or so from the ferrule. Holding the brush upright, slap the wall with the heel of the bristles (closest to the ferrule). Work from the bottom to the top of the surface.

STEEL COMBING
BASE: Golden Harvest
2157-20
GLAZE: Leather Saddle Brown
2100-20

**PLASTERING WITH
A SPATULA**
BASE: White
GLAZE: Deep Ochre 1048

STEEL COMBING
Holding the metal comb between your thumb and four fingers, pull the teeth through the wet glaze. Wipe the comb off periodically with a damp rag.

PLASTERING WITH A SPATULA
Holding the spatula in the crook of your hand, pick up a small amount of Venetian plaster. Holding the spatula at an acute angle to the walll, use short strokes in various directions to spread on a thin coat.

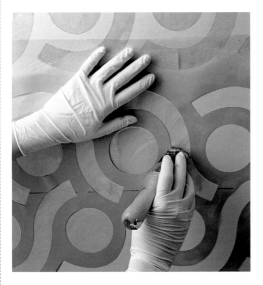

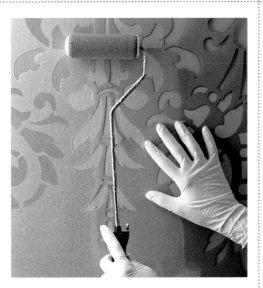

STENCILING WITH A STENCIL BRUSH

Hold a stencil brush loaded with very little paint (almost dry) perpendicular to the surface. Press the flat bristles into the stencil template and move the brush in a circular swirling motion until the pattern is filled with paint.

STENCILING WITH A FOAM ROLLER

Run the roller across an artist's paper palette to offload the excess paint, then roll lightly onto the stencil template. Keep the roller as dry as possible to minimize leaking under the stencil.

STENCILING WITH A STENCIL BRUSH
BASE: Lookout Point 1646
GLAZE: Slate Blue 1648

STENCILING WITH A FOAM ROLLER
BASE: Blue Bayou 801
GLAZE: Blue Toile 748

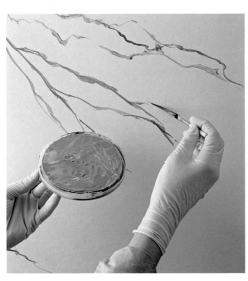

MARBLING WITH A VEINING BRUSH

Hold the brush near the tip of the handle between your forefinger, middle finger, and thumb. Keep your grasp loose and flexible: The less controlled your mark, the more natural the veining will appear.

DETAILING WITH A SCRIPT LINER

Hold the script liner midway down the handle between your thumb, forefinger, and middle finger. Keep your wrist flexible and your grip light; allow the brush to glide and form its own unique mark.

MARBLING WITH A VEINING BRUSH
BASE: White
GLAZE: Adirondack Green 453

DETAILING WITH A SCRIPT LINER
BASE: Stuart Gold HC-10
GLAZE: White

paint essentials

WHAT ARE VOCS?
Volatile organic compounds, or VOCs, are carbon containing chemical compounds that readily evaporate into the atmosphere and contribute to the formation of smog. Common examples of products which emit VOCs include gasoline, mineral spirits, alcohol, nail polish, and paint. VOCs in coatings are being reduced through regulation and manufacturer's initiatives.

The key ingredients in paint are pigment, for opacity and color; binder (resin), the "glue" solution that binds the pigment to a surface; and solvent liquid mix, which keeps the paint in a liquid form. Pigments come from a variety of natural and synthetic sources: White pigments are predominantly titanium dioxide and zinc oxide. Colored pigments are derived from naturally occurring iron oxides (reds, browns, umbers) or are synthetically produced (bright reds, blues, greens, yellows, etc.). Generally, more expensive paints use higher-quality grades of these three key ingredients. The result is better coverage ("hiding"), more durability, and less color fading.

PRIMERS

A primer is the first coat for all unpainted or untreated surfaces, sealing the surface so moisture can't penetrate. It also provides a foundation of even porosity that helps the subsequent coat of paint, especially glossy finishes, cover and adhere evenly. Some colors require a specific primer to achieve an accurate color match.

Surfaces that are already painted also benefit from a coat of primer, especially those that are excessively worn or simply old—multiple layers of latex paint become absorbent over time if the surface isn't resealed. You should also prime surfaces that have been, or will be, painted in a dark color so that the new color isn't compromised. (Tinting the primer with the new color will help the topcoat cover better.)

LATEX PAINT Latex paint is by far the most popular choice for interior finishes. Since it is water-based (meaning the solvent is water), it is

particularly easy to use: It has relatively little odor, cleanup requires just soap and water, on-the-job errors are easily wiped off with a damp rag, and the drying time is relatively quick. It's nonyellowing, retains its color longer than oil-based-paints, and is low in volatile organic compounds (VOCs).

In most decorative finishes involving a glaze a slow drying time is required to manipulate the glaze and latex's fast drying can be a drawback. In these cases, you should work in smaller areas at a time and add an extender to the glaze mixture that slows drying time (see page 163).

OIL OR ALKYD PAINT Oil paints (also known as alkyds) dry to a hard, stain-resistant finish. Although these solvent-based paints are quickly becoming less available due to clean air (VOC) regulations, they are still preferred by some decorative painters because they dry more slowly than latex, offering a longer window in which the paint can be manipulated and in which brushstrokes have time to level off and disappear.

Oil-based paints tend to yellow in color significantly. And they rely on solvents, both as an essential ingredient and for cleaning brushes and tools. These substances, which are VOCs, are volatile, flammable, and difficult to dispose of. Oil paints are increasingly being used as "specialty" products in smaller and smaller quantities.

PAINT FINISHES (SHEENS)

Interior paints come in a wide variety of finishes, or sheens, from a flat, nonreflective surface to a high-gloss shine. Generally, the higher the gloss, the more durable the finish, although there are new matte formulas that now stand up to washing as well as their shinier cousins.

HIGH GLOSS The shiniest finish available, high gloss is often used to draw the eye to a specific architectural feature, such as a door or mantel. But high-gloss finishes tend to be less forgiving of surface imperfections and may show brush strokes. And a high-gloss finish under a decorative glaze coat can prove tricky: If there is too much slide, the glaze may not adhere well. If you want to use gloss as a base coat, test the gloss and glaze coat combination on a sample board first to see how they interact.

SEMI GLOSS Durable and shiny without looking wet, semi gloss is the most common choice for doors, windows, trim, and even walls in high-traffic areas such as stairwells. The smooth, reflective surface stands up to scuffs, stains, and scrubbing and is a practical choice for spots that invite touching, like banisters and doorjambs. Most of the glazing base coats in this book are either semi gloss or satin because they provide the best surface for a glaze.

SATIN (LOW-LUSTRE) The surface finish very much resembles the sheen of satin fabric, hence the name. As a stand-alone finish, satin finishes are well suited for kitchens, bathrooms, and trim. Along with semi gloss, this is a preferred base coat under latex glazes, providing just the right sheen for the glaze to glide on.

PEARL Named for the soft, shimmering luster of a cultured pearl, these finishes are elegant and softly reflective in a way that hides surface imperfections. They can be used as a base coat for all types of glazes.

EGGSHELL Slightly shinier than flat or matte but with less luster than a pearl finish, eggshell holds up well to washing. When you look directly at an eggshell finish, it almost appears flat, but when you view the finish from the side (such as looking down a hallway), you will see a soft shine or sheen. A popular choice for interior walls.

MATTE This velvety, flat finish with just the slightest trace of a shine is a stylish alternative to a dead flat paint on walls. Some of the newer formulas produce a soft, nonreflective surface that is just as washable and durable as a semi-gloss, making this a perfect choice for areas where you want a flat finish that can be easily cleaned. It is also a good choice for making bumps, cracks, and other imperfections less noticeable.

WHEN TO PAINT
The ideal temperature for interior painting is around 70° Fahrenheit, with about 50 percent humidity and adequate ventilation.

The rest is common sense: Don't paint on a day when it's too cold or rainy to open any windows; by the same token, don't start work in the middle of a soaring heat wave. Take stock of the drying times your various paint products require (consult the manufacturer's labels) and plan your schedule accordingly.

WHEN IS IT DRY?
Paints may dry to the touch in 30 minutes but take several hours or longer to fully cure. Only then can tape or a glaze be applied to the surface. If you apply a finish over a coat that isn't fully cured, it may end up blistering or peeling over time.

paint essentials

SAMPLE SIZES
Paint samples are the perfect size for coloring many glaze recipes. Keep with the 4:1 formula: just mix one 2-ounce paint sample with 8 ounces of glazing liquid to make 10 ounces of glaze.

FLAT Flat finishes are often used on ceilings, where the no-shine paint absorbs light rather than reflecting it, masking any surface imperfections. It tolerates gentle washing but not scrubbing, so it's not a good choice for walls in high-traffic areas or children's rooms. If you're applying a decorative glazed finish to a ceiling, start with a semi-gloss base coat instead. The glaze coat will cut down on the sheen, resulting in a matte or eggshell finish.

OTHER PRODUCTS

ARTIST'S ACRYLICS Artist's acrylics are mostly used in mural and stencil work, freehand designs, and trompe l'oeil effects. They can be applied to any primed or painted surface, are colorfast and durable, and dry quickly—a benefit when you need to layer on detail for a complex design. Dabbed on with a stencil brush, artists' acrylics are thick enough to stay within the stencil borders, rather than bleed underneath. Since stenciling often requires many colors in small amounts, some painters use acrylic craft paints, available in small plastic squeeze-tip containers. Craft acrylics come in a wide variety of colors and boast a thick, creamy consistency that makes them easy to work with.

JAPAN COLORS Japan colors are finely ground, lead-free pigments mixed into a fast-drying alkyd base. The colors are rich and intense, have a luxurious silky quality, and blend well. They dry to a velvety matte finish in an hour, making them ideal for layering on detail and color (they are often used in marbleizing, wood graining, and stenciling), and they can be applied to any previously painted or primed surface. They provide better coverage than latex paints, and some professionals feel Japan colors have better flow and a smoother finish (no visible brush strokes when dry) than acrylics. Because they are oil-based, Japan colors require the use of mineral spirits for cleanup.

SOLVENTS AND THINNERS Solvents and thinners serve multiple purposes: They give paint fluidity and transparency; they can erase parts of a design you're not happy with and clean up fresh spills; and they can remove dried paint.

For water-based paints, the solvents are denatured alcohol or water. In oil-based systems, the solvents include turpentine, mineral spirits, and "odorless" paint thinner, all of which are volatile.

In faux finishing, solvents are also used to cut through the glaze layer to reveal the color underneath. In marbling and some other effects, for example, spattering denatured alcohol onto a lightly glazed surface that has been cheese-clothed off to even out and remove some of the glaze, then lightly dragging a hake brush across the surface to soften the edges, leaves a negative spray spatter of holes in the glaze, revealing the base coat color.

UNIVERSAL TINTS Available in commercial paint supply stores, universal tints are used to add color to glaze, paint (both latex and oil), or a mixture of the two. The highly concentrated colorants come in an array of earth tones and natural colors, such as burnt umber and raw sienna, which can then be mixed to create other, more complex shades. Professionals sometimes prefer universal tints rather than paint to color a glaze, because only a few drops of tint are necessary. But add too much of this pure pigment and your glaze will became hard to handle and will not dry properly.

For the beginner, mixing tints to create the desired color is truly a process of trial and error. It can get messy, and unless you keep accurate records, you won't be able to mix the exact same color should you run out of glaze before your job is complete. Nonprofessionals are better off using paint as a colorant instead. It's easier to choose a specific shade and have the paint store custom-mix it for you than to attempt a mix on your own. All the step-by-step techniques in this book used paint rather than universal colorants in the glazes.

VARNISHES Use varnishes to protect decorative designs on floors, counters, and other surfaces that get a lot of use. Acrylic polyurethane is a water-based varnish that is quick to dry and is noted for its toughness and resistance to yellowing. It is best suited for floor areas that get heavy use, and wherever sheen and durability are needed. Cleanup is easy, and most jobs can be completed in one day. Use these varnishes over decorative glazed walls or wherever you need to be able to wash the surface. Murals are almost always treated with an acrylic topcoat.

VENETIAN PLASTER Formulated with either acrylic resin or naturally occurring limestone, modern water-based Venetian plasters dry hard while maintaining flexibility. When fully cured, they have the toughness and color-fastness that acrylic polymers provide. Developed for professional installers, these Venetian plasters are part of a system that includes specially formulated foundation coats and an acrylic sealant topcoat. They come in several finishes, some designed for high-traffic areas, with high scratch and stain resistance. For decorative artists, many of the products can be used on top of each other to create different finishes and color combinations.

GLAZING LIQUID Glazing liquid is effectively a paint with no pigment (though it looks white in the can). Mixed with a coloring agent, such as an interior paint, artist's acrylic paint, or universal tint, it makes the glaze used in many decorative finishes, from faux finishes to color washes.

The most generally recommended formula for a latex glaze is four parts glaze to one part paint; you can increase the translucence by adding more glazing liquid, glaze extender (see page 00), or small amounts of water. Most finishes pictured in this book were created with a glaze consisting of a commercial glazing liquid and interior paint, occasionally thinned with a small amount of water. (Water has no binder of its own, so the more you add to the glaze, the weaker the binder eventually becomes, resulting in a glaze that can be washed off. Such surfaces can be sealed with a protective varnish coat.)

Glazes usually dry to a matte or at most eggshell finish; if you want a higher sheen, such as when you are simulating marble or wood, apply a finishing coat of gloss varnish.

Oil-based and alkyd glazing mediums are tinted with oil paint and thinned with paint thinner. The glaze/paint ratio is the same as for a latex

glaze, but there is no need for a glaze extender as oil paints dry much more slowly. Many painters, both professional and amateur, still prefer them, despite concerns about yellowing and environmental issues.

GLAZE EXTENDERS Because latex-based glazes dry quickly, you'll usually need to add glaze extender to them to ensure they remain open and workable (see keeping a "wet edge," page 63). An extender shouldn't affect the color, opacity, or transparency of the glaze, just its "open time." The exact amount of extender needed in a mix depends on a number of variables, from the complexity of the technique to the size of the work area (the smaller the area you work at a time the less extender). The most reliable way to find the best mix is to experiment with the technique on sample boards and add extender as necessary.

SPECIALTY GLAZES A combination of a latex glaze with specially treated mica particles, pearlescent glazes and gold, silver, copper and bronze metallic finishes add a lustrous, luminous quality to walls and ceilings. They can be applied with a high volume low-pressure (HVLP) spray or they can be sponged, striéd, or combed on top of a base color for a highly shimmering effect. Your paint retailer can help you determine the best color to pair with a given pearlescent tint to create the effect you desire. If you want to create a custom color outside of the range available, use universal tints (see page 160)—paint will overpower the pearlescent effect. With all these specialty glazes, follow the manufacturer's instructions closely,

taking special note of recommended primers and extenders.

SPECIALTY PAINTS Chalkboard paint now means you can have a wipe-off writing surface almost wherever you want to keep track of lists and appointments or as a surface for children's drawings. It can be applied like any other latex paint anywhere from pantry doors to home offices to playrooms.

Stenciled or rubber stamped on top of a base color, glow-in-the-dark paint is almost invisible by day. but at night the stenciled pattern—of moons and stars or nursery rhyme animals, for example—reveals itself.

Glitter paint is also a translucent product designed to go over a base color. It can be used as an allover wash, to add sparkle to a wall or ceiling, or stenciled selectively in a pattern or border around a room.

THIS PAGE
Ideal for stenciled moons, stars, and night time sprites, glow in the dark paint adds another dimension to a child's bedroom when the lights are out.

OPPOSITE
The kitchen of this Chicago loft is a collection of innovative surfaces, from stainless steel counters, to sandblasted mirror glass on the cabinets, to the handsome (and handy) blackboard wall. Designer Lisa Ewing chose black over green chalkboard paint because she loved the cheerful impact of colored chalk against the black slate.

general equipment

- No matter how neat your work habits or how well organized you are, decorative painting is by its very nature pretty messy work. Always clear out a good-size workspace for yourself and your equipment, and have a large number of plastic containers and rags on hand.

- To mask large areas of wall or ceiling space, try taped plastic drop cloths. These thin sheets of folded plastic with masking tape along one edge can be handy for shielding a broad stretch of wall space from a messy technique.

BUCKETS WITH LIDS, MIXING STICKS Use a two-gallon paint bucket for mixing glaze/paint blends and adding colorants, etc. A two-gallon size is also good for rinsing sponges, rags, and other tools. Keep a one-gallon bucket with fresh water nearby for cleaning up of spills and spatters on the spot without having to go to a utility sink. Have a good supply of clean wooden stir sticks on hand—paint needs to be stirred frequently to keep pigment from separating.

CUTTING TOOLS Single-edged safety razor blades are the perfect tool for scraping paint off glass and to hold against a piece of tape to cut the perfect 45-degree angle when you're masking off corners. Keep at least half a dozen blades around for all these odd jobs. Scissors are always handy for cutting tape, plastic sheeting, rolls of paper floor protection, rags, and other materials.

DROP CLOTH Quality canvas drop cloths absorb spills, protect floors from paint splatters and ladder scratches, and provide good traction underfoot.

LATEX GLOVES For water-based products, gloves aren't essential, but they do make clean-up a lot quicker and easier, especially with effects such as mottling and ragging where you'll get a lot of paint on your hands. Rubber or chemical gloves are better choices if you're using oil-based glazes and thinners.

MEASURING DEVICES Use a measuring tape at the beginning of a job to determine the square footage; you'll need this figure to calculate the amount of paint and glazing liquid required for the job; a calculator will speed the arithmetic. Once work is underway, you'll need the measuring tape, a carpenter's level, and rulers to mark out any pattern you're creating, such as a grid or stripes, before taping. Keep a few sharp pencils on hand as well.

PAINTER'S "FIVE-IN-ONE" This multi-purpose tool is a handy opener for cans, a scraper for cleaning rollers, and a substitute for your mislaid razor blade. The built-in cutter can cut tape at corners or remove peeling or dried paint.

RAGS You can never have enough clean cloth rags. Use them to clean up spills and spatters, correct painting errors, and wipe off brushes and combs during techniques.

If you're rag-rolling a wall, the texture of the rag will affect the final finish, so make sure you have enough rags of the same material to finish the job; you will need to use a fresh one as each rag becomes saturated.

Rags used with water-based mediums can be rinsed out and allowed to air-dry for reuse. *Rags and tools soaked in oil paint, thinner, or stain can spontaneously ignite under certain conditions, so they present a special hazard. They should be thoroughly dried before they are put in the trash or immersed in water until they can be disposed of safely.*

RESPIRATOR OR DUST MASK Always wear an NIOSH approved dust mask or respirator when sanding.

ROLLER TRAY Choose an angled metal tray and use disposable plastic liners for extra-fast cleanup.

SANDPAPER AND TACK CLOTH

Rough areas that have been patched and primed benefit from a light sanding with 120- or 150-grit sandpaper before they are painted. Smooth, previously painted surfaces, such as trim work painted with oil paint, may need a light sanding to help the new paint coat adhere; use 100-grit sandpaper to give these surfaces some tooth. Always wipe off the sanding dust with a tack cloth before painting.

SMALL PLASTIC CONTAINERS

Sealable pint- and quart-size plastic containers with lids are useful for storing different glaze colors once they are mixed. Label each container with a permanent marker so you know exactly what it contains.

SNAP LINE AND PLUMB BOB
For larger areas, such as entire walls or floors, use a chalk snap line to mark straight lines between two points. Snap lines require two people to stretch the string between two measured points; when the string is snapped, a chalk print is deposited on the surface. Make sure the snap line uses white chalk that can be wiped off with a damp cloth or dry brush before painting; some models leave an indelible line.

Use a plumb bob or plumb line to mark vertical lines, such as for painting decorative stripes. For smaller areas, the best tool for keeping things straight and even are the laser levels found at all home improvement stores.

STEPLADDER
Look for a sturdy stepladder with a paint shelf or hook for a paint bucket. Never perch on the very top or attempt to balance full buckets or cans on a step. When you find yourself leaning over or stretching to reach hard-to-paint areas, get down and move the ladder instead.

TAPE
Green or blue low-tack painter's tape is used for taping off decorative grids and patterns, masking small areas, and attaching stencils to walls; it comes in widths ranging from $\frac{3}{4}$ins to 3ins. Drafting tape in narrow widths is also invaluable when creating grout lines for faux stone finishes.

Despite the name, never use standard masking tape when painting—it can pull fresh paint off the wall.

THIN PLASTIC SHEETING
Use to drape over furniture or tape to adjacent surfaces to protect them from inadvertent splatters. Plastic isn't a good choice underfoot—it rips easily, won't absorb spills, and can be dangerously slippery; use a canvas drop cloth instead.

tips

- To remove tape, fold the edge back on itself and pull gently downward, rather than straight out from the wall. Avoid taping out more than you can finish in one day; left on too long, even painter's tape can pull paint off, especially from fresh finishes.

safety, cleanup and storage

SAFETY GUIDELINES Following proper safety procedures when painting helps protect you, your home, and the environment. For your own personal safety:

• Wear protective eyewear, such as plastic glasses or goggles, particularly when painting a ceiling.

• Wear protective clothing and latex gloves when handling oil paints, solvents, and glazes.

• *Rags and tools soaked in oil paint, thinner, or stain can spontaneously ignite under certain conditions, so they present a special hazard. They should be thoroughly dried before they are put in the trash or immersed in water until they can be disposed of safely.*

• Wear an NIOSH approved lightweight dust or particle mask when sanding or a respirator when working with solvents. Both are available at hardware and paint stores.

• Make sure the room is well ventilated, with several open windows.

• Never work with solvents, solvent-based paints, or their clean-up supplies near an open flame or pilot light (that includes a furnace and water heater).

• Protect floors with good-quality canvas drop cloths—thin plastic sheets can be extremely slippery.

LEAD PAINT SAFETY Lead compounds were used in paints for hundreds of years and were quite common up to the first half of the twentieth century. In 1978, the federal government prohibited the use of lead in the manufacture of architectural coatings.

Old paint that is adhering well and isn't cracking, flaking, or chalking does not present a hazard even if it contains lead. However, if old paint is sanded, scraped, or otherwise disturbed, dust is generated, which may pose a lead hazard. Any work on homes built prior to 1978 requires special precautions to protect both the occupants and workers. Dust or fumes containing lead can cause serious injury and are especially dangerous to children and pregnant women.

Controlling exposure to lead or other hazardous substances requires the use of proper protective equipment, such as a properly fitted respirator (NIOSH approved), and proper work practices, including containment of dust and fumes and careful cleanup of the work area.

For additional information, contact the USEPA Lead Information Hotline at 1-800-424-LEAD or www.epa.gov/lead, or visit your local independent paint retailer.

PAINT DISPOSAL Disposal of any liquid paint is a problem for sanitation collectors and for the landfill, and most municipalities have strict rules against it. Empty paint cans are no problem—just let them dry in the air for a few days, then dispose of them along with your trash. Better yet, take advantage of recycling programs for steel and plastic in your community. Cans containing a small amount of paint can be left to dry out, or the paint can be poured into a cardboard box containing shredded paper or cat litter and left to dry. Once dry, the whole container can be disposed of with your trash. Cans containing too much paint to dry efficiently should be sealed and stored until your next household hazardous waste collection day, which most municipalities hold once or twice a year. However, consider retaining enough paint for touch-ups or donating quantities of leftover paint to a community-based organization that may need it.

Rags and tools soaked in oil paint, thinner, or stain can spontaneously ignite under certain conditions, so they present a special hazard. They should be thoroughly dried before they are put in the trash or immersed in water until they can be disposed of safely.

GENERAL SAFETY Note Always wear proper protective clothing, and follow the manufacturer's recommendations for the correct use and handling of equipment, paints, stains, and all other materials mentioned in this book.

For additional product and application information, please call Benjamin Moore Customer Service at 1-800-6-PAINT-6 or visit www.benjaminmoore.com.

For the look of aged wood, Alpha Workshops used the first glaze to strié the entire surface, including the molding (strié the vertical molding vertically, the horizontal molding horizontally). To "antique" the inner part of the molding and the wall near it and give it the effect of accumulated paint and age, the second glaze was faded up and into the rest of the wall. Lastly, paint was spattered on to create the look of wormholes.

BASE: Linen White
GLAZE 1: Norwich Brown HC-19
GLAZE 2: Jamesboro Gold HC-88
SPATTER: Jamesboro Gold HC-88

resources

Brushes, tapes, tools, instructional materials, and other supplies for decorative painting are sold at paint and hardware stores, art supply stores, and craft stores nationwide. The internet is an effective way to search for educational material and hard-to-find items.

PRECEDING PAGE
Designer Arthur Dunnan at Jed Johnson got the idea for this whimsical bathroom in Woodstock, Vermont, from a collection of paper silhouettes he spotted at a flea market. The "family" portraits stenciled on the wall by James Boyd and Anne Reath look serious and formal from a distance, but a closer inspection reveals tongue-in-cheek dogs and wigged caricatures. The mirror is an antique embellished with more stenciled profiles.

BENJAMIN MOORE & CO.
www.benjaminmoore.com
View new products and colors, jot down your favorites in your personal notebook page, then use the paint calculator to find out how much paint you'll need. This site helps you keep track of all your interior painting projects. Use the store locater to find a retailer near you.

DICK BLICK
www.dickblick.com
Stencil brushes, sea sponges, posterboard.

FAUX EFFECTS WORLD
www.fauxfx.com
Everything for the professional decorative painter.

THE FAUX FINISHING SHOPPE
www.fauxfinishingshop.com
Cheesecloth by the bolt; all types of safe-release painting tapes; stretchy tape for masking off curved designs; posterboard and styrene sheets for making sample boards; brushes and other tools.

JERRY'S ARTARAMA
www.jerrysartarama.com
Specialty brushes, stipplers, sea sponges, combs.

NEW YORK CENTRAL ART SUPPLY
www.nycentralart.com
Brushes and other supplies.

PAINTING A DREAM
www.paintingadream.com
Large stencils for borders and wallpaper effects in various designs. Stencils are cut from 7.5 mil Mylar film, making them suitable for plaster work as well as paint.

PLAID
plaidonline.com
Large selection of craft foam stamps, also stencil brushes, sea sponges, combs, and stencil plastic.

ROYAL DESIGN STUDIO
royaldesignstudio.com
Large stencil collection including borders, all-over patterns, and individual motifs. Stencil brushes and paints, faux finish supplies.

RUBBER STAMPEDE
www.rubberstampede.com
Rubber sponge stamps for borders and repeat prints in a variety of designs.

THE STENCIL LIBRARY
www.stencil-library.com
Large stencil collection, everything from Art Deco to Medieval to children's designs, as well as stenciling accessories, applicators and other materials.

THIS PAGE
Ragging
BASE: Folk Art 528
GLAZE: Thyme 2148-20

designer directory

SAMUEL BOTERO ASSOCIATES
Samuel Botero
215 East 58th St., Suite 6B
New York, NY 10022
(212) 935-5155
www.botero.com

BRIAN MURPHY INC.
Brian Murphy
147 E. 37th St.
New York, NY 10016
(212) 545-0036
brian@brianmurphyinc.com
www.brianmurphyinc.com

COLIN COWIE
568 Broadway
Suite 705
New York, NY 10012
www.colincowie.com

CRAIG NEALY ARCHITECTS LLP
Craig Nealy
49 West 38 Street, Floor 12a
New York, NY 10018
(917) 342-0060
www.craignealy.com

MARK CHRISTOFI INTERIOR DESIGN
Mark Christofi
348 Park St., Suite East 106
North Reading, MA 01864
(978) 664-8354

DAVENPORT & CO.
Isabelle Vanneck
(203) 629-9181
davnportco@aol.com

DIAMOND & BARATTA DESIGN
270 Lafayette Street
New York, NY 10012
www.diamondbarattadesign.com

DRAKE DESIGN ASSOCIATES
Jamie Drake
315 East 62 Street, 5th Floor
New York, NY 10021
(212) 754-3099
www.drakedesignassociates.com

EASTRIDGE DESIGN
Katie Eastridge
215 Nassau Street
Princeton, NJ 08542
(609) 921-2827
www.eastridgedesign.com

EWING DESIGN GROUP
Lisa Ewing
1867 North Bissell Street, Suite A
Chicago, IL 60614
(312) 493-6801
www.designewing.com

CAROLYN GUTTILLA
Carolyn Guttilla
(212) 439-6673
(973) 386-1925
carolynguttilla@verizon.net

JED JOHNSON & ASSOCIATES
Arthur Dunnam
32 Sixth Avenue
New York, NY 10013
(212) 707-8989
www.jedjohnson.com

JEFFERS DESIGN GROUP
Jay Jeffers
550 15 Street, Suite 39
San Francisco, CA 94103
(415) 934-8088
and
11601 Wilshire Boulevard, Suite 500
Los Angeles, CA 90025
(310) 235-1423
www.jeffersdesigngroup.com

JAMES LUMSDEN
(310) 276-5640

LYNN MORGAN DESIGN
Lynn Morgan
147 Rowayton Avenue
Rowayton, CT 06853
(203) 866-1940
www.lynnmorgandesign.com

MARTHA ANGUS INC.
Martha Angus
55 East 93 Street, Suite 2A
New York, NY 10022
(917) 684-5864
and
1017 Bush Street
San Francisco, CA 94109
(415) 931-8060
www.marthaangus.com

MARTYN LAWRENCE-BULLARD
DESIGNS
Martyn Lawrence-Bullard
658 North Crescent Heights
Los Angeles, CA 90048
(323) 512 2959
www.martynus-tripp.com

MILES REDD LLC
Miles Redd
77 Bleecker Street, Suite C111
New York, NY 10012
(212) 674-0902
www.milesredd.com

KATIE RIDDER
432 Park Avenue South, 11th Floor
New York, NY 10016
(212) 779-9080
www.katieridder.com

SARA BENGUR INTERIORS
Sara Bengur
601 West 26 Street, Suite 1509
New York, NY 10001
(212) 226-8796 tel
(212) 226-8267 fax
www.sara bengur.com

G. P. SCHAFER ARCHITECT
270 Lafayette Street, Suite 1302
New York, NY 10012
(212) 965-1355
www.gpschafer.com

STEVEN MILLER DESIGN STUDIO
550 15th Street, Suite 39
San Francisco, California 94103
Phone (415) 934-8088
www.stevenmillerdesignstudio.com

SUZANNE KASLER INTERIORS
Suzanne Kasler
425 Peachtree Hills Avenue, 21B
Atlanta, GA 30305
(404) 355-1035
www.suzannekasler.com

TURCK-NUGENT DESIGN STUDIO
John Turck
(323) 650-3077
johnturck@aol.com

ZG DESIGN
Zina Glazebrook
5 Robin Lane
Box 604
Shelter Island, NY 11964
(631) 749-5058

decorative painters

EVERGREENE PAINTING STUDIOS, INC.
Robin Roi
450 West 31st Street, 7th Floor
New York, NY 10001-4608
(212) 244-2800 phone
(212) 244-6204 fax
www.evergreene.com

ALPHA WORKSHOPS, INC.
Kenneth Wampler
245 West 29th Street, 14th Floor
New York, NY 10001
(212) 594-7320 phone
(212) 594-4832 fax
www.alphaworkshops.org

DAVID ANDERSON
(917) 854-3380

JAMES BARRY
233 Rock Road, #224
Glen Rock, NJ 07452
(800) 522-4086
jay@jamesbarryonline.com
www.jamesbarryonline.com

BENEVILLE STUDIOS INC.
Michael Beneville
160 Charles Street
New York, NY 10014
michael@beneville.com
(917) 405-3774

BOYD REATH STUDIO
James Boyd/Anne Reath
336 West 37th Street, 9th floor
New York, NY 10018
(212) 967-8549

EVA BUCHMULLER
(718) 797 0854

DEAN BARGER STUDIOS
Dean C. Barger
111 E 14th Street, #202
New York, NY 10003
(917) 544-9341
info@deanbarger.com
www.deanbarger.com

SHELLY DENNING
(203) 912-4145
(203) 461-8655

DOMINIC FUSCO STUDIOS
5763 Park Avenue
Fairfield, CT 06825
(203) 374-3465
www.dominicfuscostudios.com

HARITZ BARNET
Jean Carrau
(914) 835-0495

IMURI DESIGN
June Eng and Patrizio Paes
107 Horatio Street
New York, NY 10014
917-488-0843
SHOWROOM:
SPACE107
212-206-7599

KATHERINE JACOBUS
katherinejacobus@aol.com
(415) 241 9331

SCARLETT JIMISON
(404) 403 0981

ADAM LOWENBEIN
Adam@Lowenbein.com
(917) 836-1585

LISA AND STEPHEN LONGWORTH
(973) 886-2858

MATTHEW MENGER
matthewmengerart@mac.com

CHRIS PEARSON
home (212) 334-3930
cell (646) 567-6892

SERPENTINE STUDIO
Louise Crandell
(917) 373-4392

WEIDL ASSOCIATES
(914) 636-5067

photography credits

TALLENTS HARDY
Art and Antiques
Hudson, New York
www.tallents-hardy.com

WILLEM RACKÉ STUDIO
1811 Folsom Street
San Francisco, CA 94103
(415) 252-1341 tel
(415) 252-7259 fax
studio@willemrackestudio.com
www.willemrackestudio.com

This book could not have been completed without the assistance of EverGreene Painting Studios of New York City. Founded by Jeff Greene in 1978, it is the largest architectural decorative arts studio in the United States and a leader in the conservation and restoration of architectural ornament and fine arts in historic buildings. Its Decorative Painting department has worked for commercial clients as diverse as Burberry's, Bergdorf Goodman, Saks Fifth Avenue, and the Rainbow Room, as well as many leading interior designers, including Bunny Williams and Mark Hampton. On all technical matters in PAINT STYLE, Robin Roi, director of Decorative Painting, was a patient and dedicated consultant. She and her team, Sandra Griffin and Kazuko Aida, created most of the step-by-step and sample decorative finishes.

Smallwood and Stewart would like to thank the many other decorative painters and designers who shared their work and their time to make this book possible. At Alpha Workshops, Ken Wampler and Russ van Peterson contributed generously of their time and talents. The border stencil on page 92 was designed by Philip Zweck-Bronner. Editorially, Sandy Gilbert's tireless energy and instinct for good design was invaluable, while Laurie Orseck guided everything with her usual grace and professionalism. Nancy Leonard saw Ivette Montez de Oca's design through to completion with skill and style.

All photographs by John Bessler except the following:
courtesy Martha Angus page 55.
Benjamin Moore & Co. page 163.
Paul Costello pages 120, 121.
John Ellis pages 5, 51, 52.
Pieter Estersohn pages 21, 39, 41, 42, 48, 58, 84, 116, 122.
Richard Felber pages 12, 89, 104.
Scott Frances page 50.
Dominic Fusco page 27.
Tria Giovan pages 56, 57, 134.
Elizabeth Glasgow pages 109, 111.
John Hall pages 44, 45, 107, 168.
Peter Margonelli pages 132, 133.
Joshua McHugh page 43.
Anastassios Mentis pages 82, 83, 176; courtesy *Connecticut Cottages & Gardens*.
Matthew Millman pages 47, 53.
Robert Murphy Photography, courtesy Lisa Ewing Design, page 162.
Eric Piasecki pages 54, 145; courtesy *Connecticut Cottages & Gardens*.
Eric Roth page 49.
Rene Stoeltie, courtesy G. P. Schafer Architect pages 60, 142, 143.
Tim Street-Porter page 40.
Brian Vanden Brink pages 16, 19.
William Waldron pages 102, 103.

PROP CREDITS: Cover, Page 46: Studio107, New York, NY. Page 1: round Chinese vase, Sutter Antiques, Hudson, NY. Page 2: Studio107, New York, NY. Page 59: Studio107, New York NY. Page 66 blue mohair throw, Gracious Home, New York, NY. Page 70: Swedish demilune, Dawn Hill, New Preston, CT; glass hurricanes, The Village Barn & Gallery, New Preston, CT. Page 72: pillow, ABC Carpet & Home, New York, NY; cashmere throw, Gracious Home, New York, NY; mid-century Danish vase, Birgit Antiques, Hudson, NY. Page 78: birdcage, Yellow Monkey Antiques, Cross River, NY. Page 114: chest, Duane, New York, NY. Page 113: Studio107, New York, NY. Page 124: sconce and Mexican vase, Keystone, Hudson, NY; ceramic canister, Gracious Home, New York, NY; mid-century Danish vase, Birgit Antiques, Hudson, NY. Page 128: chair, Yellow Monkey Antiques, Cross River, NY.

FOLLOWING PAGE
Designer Isabelle Vanneck used a subtle strié to give the walls of a traditional Connecticut living room a luxurious touch, reminiscent of raw silk.
BASE: Mystical Blue 792
GLAZE: Faded Denim 795